Principles of
PHYSICAL SCIENCE I

DANTES/DSST* Test Study Guide

All rights reserved. This Study Guide, Book and Flashcards are protected under the US Copyright Law. No part of this book or study guide or flashcards may be reproduced, distributed or stored in a retrieval system, or transmitted in any form or by any means, electronic, mechanical, photocopying, recording, or otherwise, without the prior written permission of the publisher Breely Crush Publishing, LLC.

© 2024 Breely Crush Publishing, LLC

*DSST is a registered trademark of The Thomson Corporation and its affiliated companies, and does not endorse this book.

971123121143

Copyright ©2003 - 2024, Breely Crush Publishing, LLC.

All rights reserved.

This Study Guide, Book and Flashcards are protected under the US Copyright Law. No part of this publication may be reproduced, distributed or stored in a retrieval system, or transmitted in any form or by any means, electronic, mechanical, photocopying, recording, or otherwise, without the prior written permission of the publisher Breely Crush Publishing, LLC.

Published by Breely Crush Publishing, LLC
10808 River Front Parkway
South Jordan, UT 84095
www.breelycrushpublishing.com

ISBN-13: 978-1-61433-685-3

Printed and bound in the United States of America.

DSST is a registered trademark of The Thomson Corporation and its affiliated companies, and does not endorse this book.

Table of Contents

Physics Content *1*
    Basic Measurements for Physical Sciences *1*
    Scientific Notation *1*
    Significant Figures *2*
    The Basics of Motion *4*
    Vectors *6*
    Newton's Laws of Motion *7*
    Falling Objects *8*
    Motion in Two Directions *9*
    Momentum *9*
    Circular Motion *10*
    Work and Energy *11*
    Simple Machines *14*
    Heat and Temperature *16*
    Heat Capacity and Specific Heat *17*
    Waves *19*
    Sound *21*
    Electromagnetic Spectrum *22*
    Light – Reflection and Refraction *23*
    Mirrors and Lenses *24*
    Static Electricity *25*
    Electric Potential *27*
    Circuits and Electric Current *27*
    Applied Electricity *29*
    Magnets *30*
    Electromagnets *31*
    Half-Cell Potentials *32*
    Nuclear Chemistry and Radioactivity *33*
Chemistry Content *35*
    Atomic Theory and Atomic Structure *35*
    Periodic Properties *38*
    Atomic Models of the Atom *40*
    Chemical Bonding *42*
    Covalent Bonding *44*
    Compounds *46*
    Naming Compounds *47*
    The Mole Concept *48*
    Liquids and Solids *52*
    Phase Changes *53*

Solutions	54
Concentrations – Molarity, Molality, and Normality	55
Colligative Properties	56
Gases	57
Gas Laws	58
Acids and Bases	60
pH and pOH	61
Precipitates and Salts	62
Common Ion Effect and Buffers	62
Writing Equations for Chemical Reactions	62
Predicting Reactions: Reaction Types	63
Balancing Chemical Equations	64
Stoichiometry	64
Limiting Reagent	66
Oxidation-Reduction Equations and Net Ionic Equations	68
Reaction Rate, Equilibrium, and Catalysts	69
Sample Test Questions	71
Test-Taking Strategies	106
Test Preparation	107
Legal Note	107

Periodic Table of the Elements

1A																	0
1 **H** Hydrogen 1.01	2A											3A	4A	5A	6A	7A	2 **He** Helium 4.00
3 **Li** Lithium 6.94	4 **Be** Beryllium 9.01											5 **B** Boron 10.81	6 **C** Carbon 12.01	7 **N** Nitrogen 14.01	8 **O** Oxygen 16.00	9 **F** Fluorine 18.00	10 **Ne** Neon 20.18
11 **Na** Sodium 22.99	12 **Mg** Magnesium 24.31	3B	4B	5B	6B	7B	8B	8B	8B	1B	2B	13 **Al** Aluminum 28.98	14 **Si** Silicon 28.09	15 **P** Phosphorus 30.97	16 **S** Sulfur 32.06	17 **Cl** Chlorine 35.45	18 **Ar** Argon 39.95
19 **K** Potassium 39.10	20 **Ca** Calcium 40.08	21 **Sc** Scandium 44.96	22 **Ti** Titanium 47.90	23 **V** Vanadium 50.94	24 **Cr** Chromium 52.00	25 **Mn** Manganese 54.94	26 **Fe** Iron 55.85	27 **Co** Cobalt 58.93	28 **Ni** Nickel 58.71	29 **Cu** Copper 63.55	30 **Zn** Zinc 65.38	31 **Ga** Gallium 69.72	32 **Ge** Germanium 72.59	33 **As** Arsenic 74.92	34 **Se** Selenium 78.96	35 **Br** Bromine 79.90	36 **Kr** Krypton 83.80
37 **Rb** Rubidium 85.47	38 **Sr** Strontium 87.62	39 **Y** Yttrium 88.91	40 **Zr** Zirconium 91.22	41 **Nb** Niobium 92.91	42 **Mo** Molybdenum 95.94	43 **Tc** Technecium (99)	44 **Ru** Ruthenium 101.07	45 **Rh** Rhodium 102.91	46 **Pd** Palladium 106.42	47 **Ag** Silver 107.87	48 **Cd** Cadmium 112.41	49 **In** Indium 114.82	50 **Sn** Tin 118.69	51 **Sb** Antimony 121.75	52 **Te** Tellurium 127.60	53 **I** Iodine 126.90	54 **Xe** Xenon 131.30
55 **Cs** Cesium 132.91	56 **Ba** Barium 137.34	71 **Lu** Lutetium 174.97	72 **Hf** Hafnium 178.49	73 **Ta** Tantalum 180.95	74 **W** Tungsten 183.85	75 **Re** Rhenium 186.21	76 **Os** Osmium 190.20	77 **Ir** Iridium 192.22	78 **Pt** Platinum 195.09	79 **Au** Gold 196.97	80 **Hg** Mercury 200.59	81 **Tl** Thallium 204.37	82 **Pb** Lead 207.19	83 **Bi** Bismuth 208.98	84 **Po** Polonium 209	85 **At** Astatine 210	86 **Rn** Radon (222)
87 **Fr** Francium (223)	88 **Ra** Radium 226.03	103 **Lr** Lawrencium (260)	104 **Rf** Rutherfordium	105 **Db** Dubnium (260)	106 **Sg** Seaborgium 263	107 **Bh** Bohrium (262)	108 **Hs** Hassium (265)	109 **Mt** Meitnerium (266)	110 **Ds** Darmstadtium (271)	111 (272)	112 (277)	113	114 (296)	115	116 (298)	117	118 (300)

| 57
La
Lanthanum
138.91 | 58
Ce
Cerium
140.12 | 59
Pr
Praseodymium
140.91 | 60
Nd
Neodymium
144.24 | 61
Pm
Promethium
(145) | 62
Sm
Samarium
150.40 | 63
Eu
Europium
151.96 | 64<
Gd
Gadolinium
157.25 | 65
Tb
Terbium
158.93 | 66
Dy
Dysprosium
162.50 | 67
Ho
Holmium
164.93 | 68
Er
Erbium
167.26 | 69
Tm
Thulium
168.93 | 70
Yb
Ytterbium
173.04 |
|---|---|---|---|---|---|---|---|---|---|---|---|---|---|
| 89
Ac
Actinium
(227) | 90
Th
Thorium
(232) | 91
Pa
Protactinium
231.04 | 92
U
Uranium
238.03 | 93
Np
Neptunium
237.05 | 94
Pu
Plutonium
(244) | 95
Am
Americium
(243) | 96
Cm
Curium
(247) | 97
Bk
Berkelium
(247) | 98
Cf
Californium
(251) | 99
Es
Einsteinium
(254) | 100
Fm
Fermium
(257) | 101
Md
Mendelevium
(258) | 102
No
Nobelium
(259) |

Color Key

s electrons	d electrons	p electrons	f electrons

PHYSICS CONTENT

Basic Measurements for Physical Sciences

meter - measure of length
liter - measure of volume
gram - measure of mass

deca-(meter, liter, gram) = 10 x the base unit   deci = 1/10 the base unit
hecto-(meter, liter, gram) = 100 x the base unit   centi = 1/100 the base unit
kilo-(meter, liter, gram) = 1000 x the base unit   milli = 1/1000 the base unit

Scientific Notation

In science, extremely large and extremely small numbers are often encountered. A simpler method of writing these numbers and denoting significant figures is called scientific notation. In scientific notation, a number is written in the standard form of **M x 10^n** where M is a single digit number from 1 to 9 and the exponent n is a positive or negative integer. If the decimal point was moved to the right to create a number from 1 to 9, then n is negative. For example, 0.00000356 would become 3.56×10^{-6}. If the decimal point was moved to the left to create a number from 1 to 9, then n is positive. For example, 144,267,000 would be 1.44567×10^8.

To add or subtract numbers in scientific notation, the exponent n must be the same for all the numbers involved. For example, to add 1.39×10^6 and 5.27×10^8 you could change 5.27×10^8 to 527×10^6 so the end result would be 528.39×10^6 or you could change 1.39×10^6 to 0.0139×10^8 and add it to 5.27×10^8 to get 5.2839×10^8 which would keep the result in correct scientific notation.

To multiply numbers in scientific notation, multiply the numbers (the M part) and then add the exponents. For example, to multiply 5.2×10^5 by 6.8×10^2, multiply $5.2 \times 6.8 = 35.36$ and then add the exponents to get $10^{5+2} = 10^7$. Now you have 35.36×10^7 which is not in correct scientific notation. To put it into correct scientific notation, move the decimal point to get 3.536×10^8.

To divide numbers in scientific notation, divide the numbers (the M part) and then subtract the exponents and move the decimal point as needed. For example to divide 5.2×10^5 by 6.8×10^2, start by dividing 5.2 by 6.8 such that $5.2/6.8 = 0.7647$ and then subtract exponents to get $10^{5-2} = 10^3$. You now have 0.7647×10^3. Move the decimal point to get 7.647×10^2.

To square a number in scientific notation, square the M value and double the exponent. For example, $(1.2 \times 10^3)^2 = 1.4 \times 10^6$. To find the square root, the exponent needs to be an even number. If it is an odd number, move the decimal one place to make M a number from 10 to 99. Then determine the square root of M and divide the exponent, n, by 2. The square root of 2.5×10^3 will be determined as the square root of 25×10^2 which is 5×10^1.

Significant Figures

Significant figures or significant digits are the digits indicating the **precision of a measurement**. There is uncertainty **only** in the last digit.

Example: You measure an object with a ruler marked in millimeters. The reading on the ruler is found to be about 2/3 of the way between 12 and 13 mm. What value should be recorded for its length?
Recording 13 mm does not give all the information that you found.
Recording 12 2/3 mm implies that an exact ratio was determined.
Recording 12.666 mm gives more information than you found.
A value of 12.7 mm or 12.6 mm should be recorded because there is uncertainty only in the last digit.

Determining the **number of significant digits** in a quantity.
1) All nonzero digits are significant and all zeros between nonzero digits are significant.
   Example: 4.521 kJ and 7002 u both have four significant digits.

2) Zeros to the left of the first nonzero digit are not significant.
   Example: 0.0002 m contains one significant digit.

3) Zeros to the right of a non-zero digit and the decimal point are significant figures
   Example: 32.500 g contains five significant digits.

4) The significance of numbers ending in zeros that are not to the right of the decimal point can be unclear, so this situation should be avoided by using scientific notation or a different decimal prefix. Sometimes a decimal point is used as a placeholder to indicate the units-digit is significant. A word like "thousand" or "million" may be used in informal contexts to indicate the remaining digits are not significant.
   Example: 12000 Pa would be considered to have five significant digits by many scientists, but in the sentence, "The pressure rose from 11000 Pa to 12000 Pa," it almost certainly only has only two.

5) Exact numbers have no uncertainty and contain an infinite number of significant digits. These relationships are definitions. They are not measurements.
   Example: There are exactly 1000 L in one cubic meter.

Rules for rounding off significant digits:

1) If the leftmost digit to be removed is a four or less, then round down. The last remaining digit stays as it was.
   Example: Round 43.4 g to two significant digits. Answer: 43 g.

2) If the leftmost digit to be removed is a six or more, then round up. The last remaining digit increases by one.
   Example: Round 6.772 g to two significant digits to get 6.8 g.

3) If the leftmost digit to be removed is a five that is followed by nonzero digits, then round up. The last remaining digit increases by one.
   Example: Rounding 18.502 g to two significant digits gives 19 g.

4) If the leftmost digit to be removed is a five followed by nothing or by only zeros, then force the last remaining digit to be even. If it is odd then round up by increasing it by one. If it is even (including zero) then it stays as it was.
   Examples: Round 18.50 g and 19.5 g to two significant digits yields 18 g and 20 g respectively.

Rules for **calculating with significant figures**:
1) For multiplication or division, the result has the same number of significant digits as the term with the least number of significant digits.
   Example: What is the volume of a compartment in the shape of a rectangular prism 1.2 cm long, 2.4 cm high and 0.9 cm deep?
   Solution: Volume = length x height x width = 1.2 cm x 2.4 cm x 0.9cm = 2.592 cm3
   Round to one significant figure and you get 3 cm3 (0.9 is one sig fig)

2) For addition or subtraction, the result has the same number of digits after the decimal point as the term with the least number of digits after the decimal point.
   Example: Volumes of 250.0 mL, 26 L, and 4.73 mL are added to a flask What is the total volume in the flask?
   Solution: Only identical units may be added to each other, so 26 L is first converted to 0.026 mL. Then for volume, add 250.0 mL + 0.026 mL + 4.73 mL. The answer of 254.756 mL is rounded to 254.8 mL because 250.0 mL has only one digit after the decimal.

3) For multi-step calculations, maintain all significant digits when using a calculator or computer and round off the final value to the appropriate number of significant digits *after* the calculation. When calculating by hand or when **writing down an intermediate value** in a multi-step calculation, maintain the first non-significant digit.

 The Basics of Motion

Dynamics is the study of the relationship between motion and the forces affecting motion. **Force** causes motion to start or to stop, to change direction, or to change speed. The **mass** of a body at rest is the same at all points in the universe because mass is the quantity of matter in the body. Earth's gravity pulls objects towards the earth. Therefore, the **weight** of an object is its mass times the acceleration due to the gravity acting upon it (**W = mg**). The units for mass are derivatives of grams (kilograms, micrograms, etc.) and the unit for weight is the Newton.

The more mass an object has, the greater the pull of gravity upon it. As the object increases its distance from the surface of the earth, the pull of gravity on it lessens. For example, a rocket triples its distance from earth so the gravitational pull on the rocket becomes 1/9 as much.

Throwing a ball puts it into motion. How fast it travels is its **speed** which is measured as the **distance** it travels divided by the **time** it took to travel that far, or **s = d/t**, which is usually kilometers per hour or meters per second. Velocity refers to both the speed and the direction of movement. A speed can be calculated for a specific distance or a specific amount of time or it can be an average speed for a total distance in a total amount of time.

Example: *A runner completes 5 kilometers of a 10K race in 20 minutes and the second half of the race in 25 minutes. What is his speed for the first half? What is his speed for the second half? What is his average speed?*

His first half speed: s = 5 km/20 min = 0.25 km/min
His second half speed: s = 5 km/25 min = 0.20 km/min
His average speed: s = 10 km/45 min = 0.22 km/min

If you are going to drive a car, you start from being parked. The car at rest is at a speed of zero. You apply pressure to the accelerator or gas pedal and the car starts moving. In less than a minute, it may reach a speed of 50 km per hour. The equation for **acceleration** is:

$$a = v2 - v1 / t$$ where v1 is the beginning velocity of 0

Likewise, when you come to a red light, you apply the brake and use the force of braking to decelerate to zero. To calculate the **deceleration**, you would use the same equation as for acceleration, but v2 would be zero instead of v1 being zero. Acceleration and deceleration are rates at which speed changes.

Acceleration is defined as the rate of change of velocity with respect to time. It is always represented with both a magnitude and a direction. Magnitude refers to the size of the change. For example, 1, 5, or 6 are representative of different magnitudes. Direction is indicted using either a positive or negative sign. Although direction is not absolute (or always the same) it is typically standard to consider up or to the right to be positive, and down or to the left to be negative unless otherwise indicated. The units of acceleration are meters per second per second, m/s/s, or meters per second squared m/s^2. Either is equally acceptable, although m/s^2 is simpler to write and is more commonly used.

As mentioned previously, acceleration is used to describe a change in velocity; however, a positive acceleration does not always indicate that an object's speed is increasing. If acceleration and velocity are in the same direction (both are positive or both are negative) then the velocity is increasing. On the other hand, if acceleration and velocity are in opposite directions (one is positive and the other is negative) then the object will move slower with time. If an object moves with a constant velocity over time, it must have an acceleration of zero.

Because acceleration is defined as the rate of change of velocity with respect to time, it must be measured as time changes. Acceleration is determined as $\Delta v/\Delta t$ (Δ is the Greek letter delta and represents change). Therefore, if an object accelerates from 3 m/s to 9 m/s in 3 seconds, its accelerates was (9-3)/3 or $2 m/s^2$.

There are a number of equations which relate acceleration to other values, such as position, time and velocity. These can be useful in doing calculations. These equations are referred to as kinematics equations. It is extremely important to remember that these equations only apply in situations where acceleration is constant. This is referred to as uniform motion, and is often assumed to make situations easier to analyze. However, if acceleration changes with time then these equations cannot be used.

The three most basic kinematics equations are (1) $v = v_o + at$, (2) $\Delta x = (1/2)at^2 + v_o t$, (3) $v = 2a(\Delta x) + v_o^2$. In the equations, v represents initial velocity (if an object starts from rest, this value can be ignored), and Δx represents change in position, or distance.

One of the most common situations in which these equations are used is when an object is in freefall, which means that it is falling under the influence of gravity. It is a common situation to use because acceleration due to gravity is always a constant 9.8 m/s² for objects of any size or mass. For an example of the kinematics equations in use, consider this problem: A block is dropped, from rest, from the top of a large building. Ignoring air friction, determine is its velocity after 3 seconds, and how far has it fallen. Because the question tells us that there is no air friction, we know that the only force is gravity, and that it must be falling with an acceleration of 9.8 m/s². Because it is falling from rest we know that initial velocity is 0. Using this information, and the fact that it tells us t=3, we can simply plug the values into the proper equations. Using the first equation we determine that $v = v_o + at = 0 + (9.8)(3) = 29.4$ m/s. Using the second equation we determine that $\Delta x = (1/2)at^2 + v_o t = (1/2)(9.8)(3^2)+(0)(3) = 44.1 + 0 = 44.1$ m.

Vectors

Quantities which have only a numeral and a unit such as mass or volume are said to be scalar quantities. When a body moves from one location to another, it is called displacement. A displacement has both a magnitude (how much) with a numeral and a unit and a direction. Quantities with magnitude and direction are vector quantities and can be represented, added, and subtracted graphically. If there are two vectors in the same direction, add them together. If there are two vectors in opposite directions, subtract the smaller from the larger.

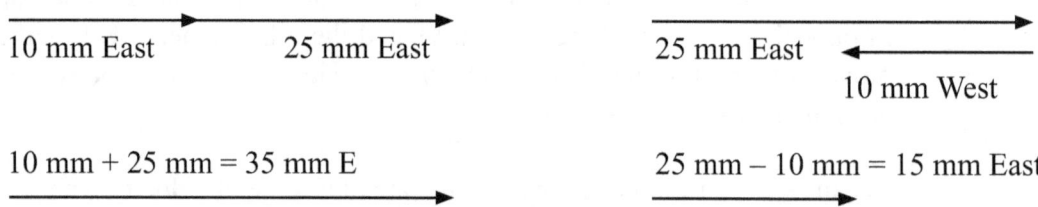

Vectors are not always this simple. However, it always helps to make a scaled drawing. If possible place the vectors head to tail. If they cannot simply be added or subtracted, you may need to use geometrical calculations based on the properties of right triangles:

Principles of Physical Science I

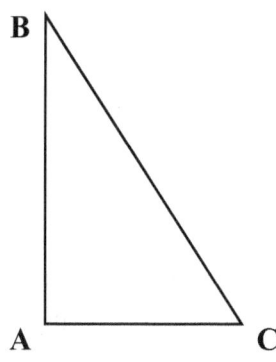

Angle A is the right angle. BC is the hypotenuse. To get the length of AB if you know angle B, use a cosine or to get the length of AB if you know angle C, use a sine. Sine or sin C = opposite side/hypotenuse = AB/BC

Cosine or cos B = adjacent side/hypotenuse = AB/BC

Tangent B or tan B = opposite side/adjacent side = AC/AB

*Displacement, velocity, and acceleration are vector quantities.

Newton's Laws of Motion

The tendency of a moving object to keep moving is called **inertia**. When you stop your car suddenly, your body keeps going forward through inertia. If a body is not moving, it takes force to make it move. This, too, is inertia. Sir Isaac Newton (1642-1727) stated three laws which explain the way objects move.

Newton's first law of motion is also called the law of inertia. It states that an object at rest will remain at rest and an object in motion will remain in motion at a constant velocity unless acted upon by an external force. For example, a sailboat floats on a lake. The sails are put up. A breeze exerts a force on the sails. The boat moves. The skipper moves the rudder right or left to change direction. The force of the water on the rudder makes the boat turn.

Newton's second law of motion states that if a net force acts on an object, it will cause the object to accelerate. The relationship between force and motion is Force equals mass times acceleration. (**F = ma**). Acceleration of an object increases as the amount of force causing the acceleration increases. Heavier objects (such as a moving van) need more force than lighter objects (such as a sports car) in order to accelerate or decelerate.

Newton's third law states that for every action there is an equal and opposite reaction. Therefore, if an object exerts a force on another object, that second object exerts an equal and opposite force on the first. For instance, a boat may be forced by the currents to drift away but an equal and opposite force is exerted by a rope holding it to a dock.

Falling Objects

If you drop a bowling ball and a tennis ball from a third story window at the same time, which will hit the ground first? If you answer that they both hit simultaneously, you are right. **Galileo** (1564-1642) thought all objects fall at the same rate so he performed several experiments to prove that. He timed the motion of a ball rolling down an inclined plane. The speed of the ball increased as it rolled down the ramp. The distance the ball traveled in each second increased. Using several balls of different masses, he discovered the speeds to be identical.

Falling objects accelerate at a rate of 9.8 meters per second squared (9.8 m/s2). That means that the speed of the falling object increases 9.8 meters per second for each second it falls. If it starts at rest, its speed the first second is 9.8 meters per second, its speed for the next second is 19.6 meters per second (2 x 9.8), its speed for the third second is 29.4 meters per second (3 x 9.8), and so forth.

Example: *If a ball is released from rest and drops for 3 sec., what is its (A) initial velocity, (B) final velocity, and (C) average velocity?*

If it is released from rest, its initial velocity is 0.
Its final velocity is 3 x 9.8 m/s² or 29.4 m/s²
Its average velocity is $v_{av} = (v + v_0) / 2 = (29.4 \text{ m/s}^2 + 0)/2 = 14.7 \text{ m/s}^2$

Example: *If a ball is dropped from a height of 54 m, how long will it take to hit the ground and what will its velocity be just before it strikes the ground?*

Given: a = 9.8 m/s², d = 54 m, and v_0 = 0
$d = v_0 t + \frac{1}{2} at^2$
54 m = 0 + ½ (9.8 m/s²)(t²)
t² = 11.0 s²
t = 3.32 seconds
$v^2 = v_0^2 + 2ad$
v² = 0 + (2)(9.8 m/s²)(54 m)
v² = 1,060 m²/s²   v = 32.6 m/s

In a vacuum there is no air, so there is no **air resistance**. However, in a normal situation you will see something like a feather drop more slowly due to air resistance, the upward force of air against the object.

Motion in Two Directions

If a stone is dropped from the mast of a moving ship, will it land on the deck of the ship below the mast or in the water direction below the point where it was dropped? The falling stone lands on the deck directly below the point from which it was dropped. Before it was released, it was moving forward at the same velocity as the ship. The stone kept its forward velocity during its fall. While falling, the stone had two velocities: forward and downward. Therefore, the path of the falling stone is curved.

When an arrow is shot horizontally from a bow, it will move in a horizontal motion but it will also be pulled down by gravity. Therefore, the archer will have to allow for the downward velocity and aim above the bulls-eye on the target.

> Example: *If a boat is to start on one side of a river flowing 3 km/hr and end up directly across river from where it started, it will have to be pointed upstream at some angle. The boat will travel 6 km/hr. What will its velocity need to be relative to the earth?*

Tan Θ = opp/adj = 3/6 = .5
Θ = 26.5° upstream
Sin Θ = opp/hyp
sin 26.5° = 3 km/hr / hyp
0.446 = 3/hyp
Hyp = 3/.446 = 6.7 km/hr

Momentum

Every object in motion has a property called momentum. The amount of momentum depends on the mass and velocity of the object: **M = mv**. As either the mass or the velocity increases, the momentum increases. The greater the momentum of an object, the more force it takes to stop it. An object at rest has zero momentum.

> Example: *Which has more momentum, a 3600-kilogram truck moving at 8 kilometers per hour or an 1800-kilogram car moving at 16 kilometers per hour? If they both move at the same speed, which one will have the greater momentum?*

For the truck: M = mv = 3600 kg x 8 km/hr = 28,800 kg-km/hr For the car: M = mv = 1800 kg x 16 km/hr = 28,800 kg-km/hr
If the car moves at 8 km: M = mv = 1800 kg x 8 km/hr = 14,400 kg-km/hr

Under the given conditions of the truck moving at 8 km/hr and the car moving at 16 km/hr, the momentum of both is identical. However, if both move at the same speed, the truck has greater momentum since it has a greater mass.

Circular Motion

Centripetal force is the force necessary to keep an object moving in a circle. It acts toward the center of a circle. A body describing uniform circular motion has a constant magnitude of velocity but a constantly changing direction. Therefore, its acceleration is **a = Δv/Δt** (Δ means "change in" and can be calculated as $v_2 - v_1$ and $t_2 - t_1$). Acceleration in circular motion is also equal to the velocity squared divided by the radius of the circle (**a = v^2/r**). Because of this, the centripetal force is:

$$F = ma = mv^2 / r$$

A model airplane is caused to move in a horizontal circle by a control wire. The wire pulls on the airplane toward the center of the circle. By Newton's third law, the airplane must exert an equal and opposite force on the wire. This force, away from the center of the circle and acting on the wire, is known as the centrifugal force. If the wire was to break or the person was to let go of the wire, the airplane would continue moving, but in a straight line tangentially to the circle in the direction its nose was headed when it was released.

When an automobile goes around a curve on a perfectly level road, friction between the tires and roadway is required to provide the necessary centripetal force. Friction is part of the idea of "for every action there is an equal and opposite reaction." If the road is coated with ice, this frictional force may be too small and the car may slide off the road. There is no force pulling the car outward along the radius. By Newton's first law, the car would continue to move indefinitely with constant velocity in the absence of any force. If there is a force toward the center of the circle which is inadequate to provide the full centripetal force, the car is accelerated toward the center but not enough to keep it on the road.

A curve is perfectly banked for a specific speed (v) of a specific vehicle when the force exerted perpendicular to its surface by the road has a horizontal component equal to the centripetal force, (mv^2/r), and a vertical component equal to the weight (mg) of the vehicle. The angle at which the road should be banked depends on the speed of the vehicle but not on its mass.

$$\tan \theta = v^2/gr$$

Work and Energy

Sir Isaac Newton is credited with many discoveries in the field of physics. Some of his most important work related to an understanding of forces. A force is a push or pull on an object which results in motion. Forces always have a direction and a magnitude. Direction is described by the sign (positive or negative). Magnitude simply refers to the strength of the force. In honor of Sir Isaac Newton, the unit that forces are measured in is the Newton (N). For reference, one Newton is the amount of force required to lift one kilogram of matter one meter.

As it relates to forces, Newton is famous for developing three Laws of Motion. Newton's second law is used to calculate force. It is that force (F) is equal to mass (m) multiplied by acceleration (a), or F=ma. Therefore, an object weighing 10 kilograms (kg), and which is accelerating at a rate of 10 meters per second squared (m/s^2) would be described as having a force of 100 N. If there are multiple forces acting on an object they would be summed together with the result being net force. For example if the same object was simultaneously being pushed in the opposite direction with a force of 50 N, the net force on the object would be 50 N (100 N – 50 N = 50 N). The formula can also be used in other arrangements, such as a=F/m or m=a/F. For example, a 5 kg box is being pulled to the left with a force of 10 N. Its acceleration must be 2 m/s^2 (a = F/m = 10/5 =2).

When a force causes an object to move, it is described using the equation for work (W). Work relates force (measured in Newtons) and distance (measured in meters). More specifically, W = (F)(d). The units of measure for work are joules (J). One joule describes one Newton of force acting on an object over a one meter distance. For an example of calculating work, consider the following scenario: a 5 kg object is moved with a force such that its acceleration is a constant 10 m/s^2 over a distance of 3 meters. From this it may be determined that the force (equal to mass times acceleration) acting on the object was 50 N. Therefore, the work must have been 150 J (50 N times 3 meters).

When work is considered over a period of time the resulting quantity is termed as power. Power describes the rate of energy transfer, which is what occurs when work is done (i.e., work causes objects to move, therefore energy must have been transferred). Power is measured in watts (W), such that one watt describes one joule per second of work. The equation for power is P = W/t. For example, the amount of power when 5 J of work is done in 2 seconds is 5 J/2 s or 2.5 watts.

Energy is the ability to exert a force through a distance or to do **work** (measured in newton-meters). **W = Fd** or **W = Fd cos Θ**. One joule is the work done when a force of one newton acts through a distance of one meter.

Example: *How many joules of work are done by a force in lifting a mass of 4 kg upward a distance of 3 m?*

Work (in joules) = force (in newtons) x distance (in meters)
F = mg = 4 kg x 9.8 m/s² = 39.2 N
W = Fd = 39.2 N x 3 m = 117.6 J

Example: *A force of 10 N is used to move a box across a horizontal floor a distance of 5 m. If the force makes an angle of 30° with the floor, how much work is done?*

W = Fd cos Θ
W = 10 N x 5 m x 0.866 = 43.3 J

Power is the work done divided by the amount of time that it took to do it. **(P = W / t)** Power is measured in joules per second or watts (W) with one watt of power being expended when one joule of work is done each second. When force and velocity are constant, the instantaneous power is equal to the average power.

Example: *An electric motor exerts a force of 400 N on a cable and pulls it a distance of 30 m in 1 min. Find the power supplied by the motor.*

P = W/t = Fd/t
P = (400 N x 30 m) / 60 s
P = 200 J/s or 200 Watts

The Law of Conservation of Energy states that energy cannot be created or destroyed; it may be transformed from one form into another, but the total amount of energy never changes. Energy comes from a variety of sources: fossil fuels, solar energy, hydroelectric power, biomass, wind, geothermal, and nuclear fission and fusion. Mass in each of these is transformed to energy through the equation $E = mc^2$ where E is energy, m is mass, and c is the speed of light. Solar energy in the form of radiation is absorbed by plants to make chemical energy through photosynthesis. This energy is stored by the plant to be used by an animal eating the plant or to be converted into light and heat many years later after the plant has become part of a peat or coal bed.

Energy can be divided into two types. The energy of motion, called **kinetic energy**, is seen in a bowling ball knocking down the bowling pins. Turning on a flashlight demonstrates the stored energy, or **potential energy**, of the batteries. Potential energy is also known as positional energy. For example, a rock at the top of a hill has potential energy but a rock in motion, rolling down the hill, has kinetic motion.

To find the kinetic energy a body possesses, we consider the work which must be done on the body in order to give it its speed. When the body is stopped, it gives up this amount of energy. Therefore, **KE = ½ mv²**.

Example: *If a 1,000 kg automobile is moving with a speed of 20 m/s, what is the kinetic energy in joules?*

$$KE = \tfrac{1}{2} mv^2$$
$$KE = \tfrac{1}{2} (1{,}000 \text{ kg})(20 \text{ m/s})^2$$
$$KE = 2 \times 10^5 \text{ J}$$

The measure of the potential energy which a body has because of its elevated position is the work done against gravity in lifting the body from some level chosen as the zero for potential energy. The upward force required is equal to the product of the weight of the body (w) and the work done in lifting the body through a height (h) such that **PE = wh = mgh**.

Example: *What is the potential energy of a 50-kg hammer of a pile driver when it is raised 4 m?*

$$PE = wh = mgh$$
$$PE = 50 \text{ kg} \times 9.8 \text{ m/s}^2 \times 4 \text{ m}$$
$$PE = 1{,}960 \text{ J} \text{ (Using significant figures PE} = 2.0 \times 10^3 \text{ J)}$$

Another important example of potential energy is the energy in a compressed spring. In general, the force that is applied to the spring is proportional to the extension of the spring: **F = ky** where k is a spring constant and y is the extension. To produce a displacement the applied force is zero at first and increases linearly to ky. The work done by the force is the product of the displacement (extension) and the average force (ky/2): $PE = \tfrac{1}{2} ky^2$.

Remember that potential energy is always measured relative to some configuration chosen as the zero. For a mass suspended from a spring, the equilibrium position is the usual choice for the zero configuration. For the gravitational potential energy, the height is measured relative to some chosen zero level. When we deal with energy of motion, the kinetic energy depends on the reference frame relative to which we measure velocities. For example, a passenger seated in an airplane traveling 1,000 m/s has no kinetic energy relative to a set of exes tied to the plane but much kinetic energy relative to axes fixed on the earth.

In many cases potential energy is transformed directly into kinetic energy. One example is water going over a dam. Another is a pendulum swinging. When the pendulum is at its highest point on the right or the left, that is its greatest potential energy and when it is vertical (its equilibrium position) it is at its greatest kinetic energy. Therefore, it goes from PE to KE to PE to KE and so forth.

<u>Example</u>: *A pendulum bob is pulled to one side until its center of gravity has been raised 10 cm above its equilibrium position. Find the speed of the bob as it swings through the equilibrium position.*

$$PE \text{ at top} = KE \text{ at bottom}$$
$$mhg = \tfrac{1}{2} mv^2 \text{ or } 2hg = v^2$$
$$(2)(0.1 \text{ m})(9.8 \text{ m/s}^2) = v^2$$
$$1.96 \text{ m}^2/\text{s}^2 = v^2$$
$$1.4 \text{ m/s} = v$$

 ## Simple Machines

A machine makes work easier by changing the direction or the distance through which a force moves. There are six types of simple machines. They are **(1) lever, (2) pulley, (3) wheel and axle, (4) inclined plane, (5) screw, and (6) wedge**.

Levers have two parts – a resistance arm and an effort arm. The effort arm is the distance from the fulcrum to the effort force. The resistance arm is the distance from the fulcrum to the resistance force. The resistance force is the weight of the object the lever will move.

There are three classes of levers. They are based on the position of the fulcrum, resistance and effort. In a first class lever, the fulcrum is between the effort and resistance.

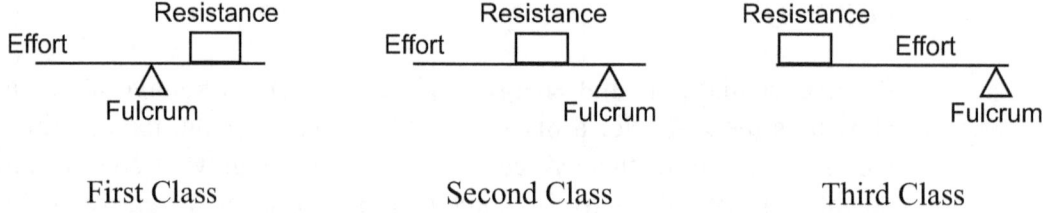

First Class   Second Class   Third Class

Examples include shoveling snow, cutting with scissors, and pulling a nail with the claw of a hammer. A second class lever has the resistance between the effort and fulcrum. Examples are a wheelbarrow, a nutcracker, and a bottle opener to open glass bottles. The third class of levers has the effort between the fulcrum and resistance. Raking leaves, hitting a baseball with a bat and using a fishing rod are examples of third class levers.

The amount by which a lever increases a force is the **mechanical advantage** for the lever. Suppose a machine produces 150 newtons of force when the effort force applied is 10 newtons. The machine multiplies the force 15 times.

Mechanical advantage (MA) = effort arm / resistance arm
MA = 150 N / 10 N = 15

A pulley makes work easier by changing the direction of a force. With a fixed pulley, the effort force is applied in one direction and the resistance moves in the opposite direction. Two or more pulleys can be used together to decrease the force needed to move an object. The mechanical advantage of a set of pulleys is about equal to the number of supporting ropes or strands.

The wheel and axle acts like a first class lever. The effort arm is the radius of the wheel. The resistance arm is the radius of the axle. The fulcrum is the center of the axle. The mechanical advantage of the wheel and axle is equal to the radius of the wheel divided by the radius of the axle.

An inclined plane (such as a ramp) is a slanted surface used to raise or lower objects. Less force is needed to lift an object using an inclined plane. However the object is moved through a longer distance than if it were moved straight up. The mechanical advantage of an inclined plane is its length divided by its height. The longer the inclined plane, the less force is needed to move the object.

A wedge is two inclined planes. A knife blade and an ax blade are wedges. The wedge moves in doing work, but a simple inclined plane does not move. A screw is also a form of inclined plane. It is like a spiral staircase with the steps wound around the center.

The useful work obtained from a machine is always less than the work put into it. Some of the input work is used to overcome friction. The ratio of work output to work input is called the efficiency of a machine. High efficiency means that a high proportion of the work put in is changed to useful work done. Low efficiency means that much of the work input is lost or not changed into useful work. Efficiency is expressed as a percent.

Percent efficiency = work output/work input x 100

Efficiency is increased by decreasing friction. Sanding rough edges or greasing bearings on machines decreases friction and helps conserve energy.

 Heat and Temperature

All matter is made of particles. These particles are in constant motion. They have kinetic energy. **Temperature** is a measure of the average kinetic energy of the particles in a material. Temperature and heat are not the same. **Heat** is the total internal energy of the material. The total kinetic energy of the particles in a material is the internal energy or heat of the material. The internal energy of a material depends on its mass as well as its temperature. A swimming pool will have more heat energy than a pan of water when the water in both is at the same temperature.

Temperature shows the tendency of a material to gain or lose heat. Objects are in thermal contact if they can affect each other's temperatures. Set a hot cup of coffee on a desk top. The two objects are in thermal contact with each other and will begin affecting each other's temperatures. Heat flows from regions of higher temperature to regions of lower temperature. The coffee will become cooler and the desktop warmer. Eventually, they will have the same temperature. When this happens, they are in **thermal equilibrium**.

Thermometers are used to measure temperature. The thermometer and the object whose temperature it is measuring are put in contact long enough for them to reach thermal equilibrium. Then the temperature can be read from the thermometer scale.

Three temperature scales are used:

Celsius: The freezing point of water is set at 0 and the steam (boiling) point is 100. The interval between the two is divided into 100 equal parts called degrees Celsius.

Fahrenheit: The freezing point of water is 32 degrees and the boiling point is 212. The interval between is divided into 180 equal parts called degrees Fahrenheit. To convert between Fahrenheit and Celsius: **F = (9/5) C + 32**

Kelvin Scale has degrees the same size as the Celsius scale, but the zero point is moved to the triple point of water. Water inside a closed vessel is in thermal equilibrium in all three states (ice, water, and vapor) at 273.15 degrees Kelvin. This temperature is equivalent to .01 degrees Celsius. Because the degrees are the same in the two scales, temperature changes are the same in Celsius and Kelvin. To convert between Celsius and Kelvin: **C = K - 273.15**.

There are a number of ways that heat is measured. In each case, the measurement is dependent upon raising the temperature of a specific amount of water by a specific amount. These conversions of heat energy and work are called the **mechanical equivalent of heat**.

The **calorie** is the amount of energy that it takes to raise one gram of water one degree Celsius. The **kilocalorie** is the amount of energy that it takes to raise one kilogram of water by one degree Celsius. Food calories are kilocalories. In the International System of Units (**SI**), the calorie is equal to 4.184 **joules**. A **British thermal unit** (**BTU**) = 252 calories = 1.054 kJ.

Heat Capacity and Specific Heat

Heat energy that is transferred into or out of a system is **heat transfer**. The temperature change is positive for a gain in heat energy and negative when heat is removed from the object or system.

The formula for heat transfer is **Q = mcDT** where Q is the amount of heat energy transferred, m is the amount of substance (in kilograms), c is the specific heat of the substance, and ΔT is the change in temperature of the substance. It is important to assume that the objects in thermal contact are isolated and insulated from their surroundings.

Heat Capacity (C_p) of an object is the amount of heat energy that it takes to raise the temperature of a unit mass of the object by one degree. Its units are kcal/(kg-C°) or J/(kg)(K). Specific heats for many materials have been calculated and can be found in tables.

Example: *Find the number of kilocalories required to raise the temperature of 0.100 kg of brass from 25 °C to 75 °C. The specific heat of brass is 0.09 kcal/ (kg-C°).*

$$Q = m\, C_p\, \Delta T$$
$$Q = 0.100 \text{ kg} \times 0.09 \text{ kcal/(kg-C°)} \times (75 - 25) \text{ C°} \quad Q = 0.45 \text{ kcal}$$

If a substance in a closed container loses heat, then another substance in the container must gain heat. A **calorimeter** uses the transfer of heat from one substance to another to determine the specific heat of the substance. Therefore, heat gained by one substance equals heat lost by the other substance. One of the most familiar methods of measuring a quantity of heat is by imparting this heat to a known mass of water and observing the change it produces in the temperature of the water.

Example: *A 0.450-kg cylinder of lead is heated to 100 °C and then dropped into a 50-g copper calorimeter containing 0.100 kg of water at 10 °C. The water is stirred until equilibrium is established, at which time the temperature of the whole system is 21.1 °C. Find the specific heat of lead.*

Heat gained by the water + Heat gained by the copper = heat lost by the lead

$$(m\ C_p\ \Delta T)_{water} + (m\ C_p\ \Delta T)_{copper} = (m\ C_p\ \Delta T)_{lead}$$
$$0.100\ kg \times 1\ kcal/(kg\text{-}C°)(21.1 - 10\ C°) + 0.050\ kg \times 0.093\ kcal/(kg\text{-}C°)(21.1 - 10\ C°) = 0.450\ kg \times (c)(100 - 21.1\ C°)$$
$$1.16 = 35.5\ (c)$$
$$0.033\ kcal/(kg)(C°) = c$$

The thermal capacity of a body is the heat required to raise the temperature of the entire body by one degree. **Thermal capacity = m C_p**.

When an object undergoes a change of phase it goes from one physical state (solid, liquid, or gas) to another. For instance, water can go from liquid to solid (freezing) or from liquid to gas (boiling). The heat that is required to change from one state to the other is called **latent heat**. Phase changes will be covered in chemistry.

Heat is transferred in three ways: **conduction, convection, and radiation**. **Conduction** occurs when heat travels through the heated solid. If you leave a metal spoon in a hot cup of coffee, the spoon will get hot. The heat moves from one end of the spoon to the other. The particles near the source have more kinetic energy and move faster than the particles farther from the hot coffee. The movement of energy up the spoon occurs as kinetic energy is transferred from particle to particle. Heat can be conducted through solids, liquids and gases.

The transfer rate is the ratio of the amount of heat per amount of time it takes to transfer heat from area of an object to another. Because the change in time is in the denominator of the function, the shorter the amount of time it takes to heat the handle, the greater the transfer rate.

Convection is heat transported by the movement of a heated liquid or gas. When liquids and gases are heated, they expand and their density decreases. The less dense material rises, causing currents that carry the heat. Warmed air rising from a heat source such as a fire or electric heater is a common example of convection. Convection ovens make use of circulating air to more efficiently cook food. Winds and ocean currents are examples of convection.

Radiation is heat transfer as the result of electromagnetic waves rather than moving particles. The sun warms the earth by emitting radiant energy.

An example of all three methods of heat transfer occurs in the thermos bottle or Dewar flask. The bottle is constructed of double walls of Pyrex glass that have a space in between. Air is evacuated from the space between the walls and the inner wall is silvered. The lack of air between the walls lessens heat loss by convection and conduction. The heat inside is reflected by the silver, cutting down heat transfer by radiation. Hot liquids remain hotter and cold liquids remain colder for longer periods of time.

The Laws of Thermodynamics help define the relationships among forms of heat, forms of energy, and work (mechanical, electrical, etc.). These laws deal strictly with systems in thermal equilibrium and not those within the process of rapid change or in a state of transition. Systems that are nearly always in a state of equilibrium are called **reversible systems**.

The First Law of Thermodynamics restates the Law of Conservation of Energy. The change in heat energy supplied to a system (Q) is equal to the sum of the change in the internal energy (U) and the change in the work (W) done by the system against internal forces. **$\Delta Q = \Delta U + \Delta W$**

The Second Law of Thermodynamics is stated in two parts:

1. No machine is 100% efficient. It is impossible to construct a machine that only absorbs heat from a heat source and performs an equal amount of work because some heat will always be lost to the environment.

2. Heat can not spontaneously pass from a colder to a hotter object. An ice cube sitting on a hot sidewalk will melt into a little puddle, but it will never spontaneously cool and form the same ice cube. Certain events have a preferred direction called the **arrow of time**.

Waves

A wave is a rhythmic disturbance which travels through space or matter. By tying a rope to a post, you can move your end of the rope up and down to create wave action. Just as waves appear to move across the rope but the particles of the rope do not move horizontally to create the waves, waves of other types (water, for example) are made of particles that oscillate up and down rather moving across a space.

Waves are classified in terms of how the motion of the individual particles of the medium is related to the movement of the wave itself. In waves produced by the rope, the particles move up and down at right angles to the direction in which the wave itself moves, making it a **transverse wave**. Each particle vibrates in simple harmonic motion with its displacement at right angles to the propagation direction. Light and other forms of electromagnetic radiation show behavior characteristic of transverse waves.

A wave motion in which the individual particles vibrate back and forth along the direction in which the wave travels is called a compressional or longitudinal wave. Sound exhibits the characteristic properties of **longitudinal waves**.

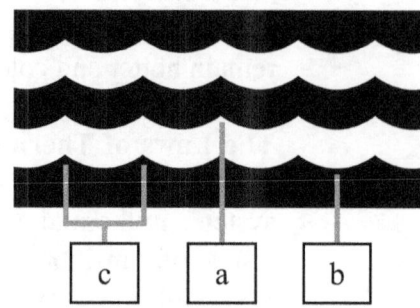

The parts of a wave are:

Crest (A) – top of the hill

Trough (B) – bottom of the valley

Wavelength (C) – the total distance from the center of one crest through one trough to the center of the next crest

Amplitude – the distance a wave rises or falls from its usual rest position

Frequency – the number of waves that pass a given point in one second expressed in hertz (Hz) which means 'per second'

As the length of a wave increases, its frequency decreases. Long waves have a low frequency while short waves have a high frequency.

The **speed of a wave** depends on the wavelength and frequency of the wave.
Speed (V) = wavelength (λ) x frequency (f)

> Example: *A tuning fork has a frequency of 256 Hz. The wavelength of the sound wave produced by the fork is about 1.3 meters. What is the speed of the wave?*
>
> $$V = \lambda f$$
> $$V = 1.3 \text{ m} \times 256 \text{ Hz}$$
> $$V = 332.8 \text{ m/s}$$

Water waves in a tank can be used as models to explain the behavior of sound, light and other energy waves. Waves that strike an object are called **incident waves**. The waves that bounce off are called **reflected waves**. The angle between the wave and a line drawn normal to the wall is the angle of incidence. A line drawn normal to the wall means the line is perpendicular to the wall at the point where the wave strikes the wall. The angle between the reflected wave and the normal is the angle of reflection. The angle of incidence equals the angle of reflection.

Refraction is the bending of waves. As water waves pass into shallow water, their wavelength becomes shorter. The speed of the waves decreases. The incident wave is bent because the whole wave is not traveling at the same speed.

One interesting characteristic of light (and of waves in general) is referred to as refraction. Refraction describes the fact that when light passes through different mediums (or materials) its speed changes. The result is that things appear to bend when they enter different substances – such as when a pencil is sitting with the top half in the water and the top half in the air. The result is that the pencil, which is straight, appears to have a bend in it. This occurs because the light moves from the pencil up through the water, and when it hits air its speed changes. This change in speed causes the light wave to bend, and the eye interprets this as a bend in the pencil. The degree of the bend depends on the specific substances involved, as refraction occurs with any medium change (e.g., glass, water, air, slime, etc.). The fact that light refracts is evidence in support of its wave-like properties.

 Sound

Sound waves are produced by a vibrating body. The vibrating object moves forward and compresses the air in front of it, then reverses direction so that the pressure on the air is lessened and expansion of the air molecules occurs. One compression and expansion creates one longitudinal wave. Sound can be transmitted through any gas, liquid, or solid. However, it cannot be transmitted through a vacuum, because there are no particles present to vibrate and bump into their adjacent particles to transmit the wave.

The vibrating air molecules move back and forth parallel to the direction of motion of the wave as they pass the energy from adjacent air molecules (closer to the source) to air molecules farther away from the source.

The **pitch** of a sound depends on the **frequency** that the ear receives. High-pitched sound waves have high frequencies. High notes are produced by an object that is vibrating at a greater number of times per second than one that produces a low note. If you have two tuning forks that produce different pitches, then one will produce sounds of a slightly higher frequency.

The **intensity** of a sound is the amount of energy that crosses a unit of area in a given unit of time. The loudness of the sound is subjective and depends upon the effect on the human ear. Two tones of the same intensity but different pitches may appear to have different loudness. The intensity level of sound is measured in decibels. Normal conversation is about 60 decibels. A power saw is about 110 decibels.

The **amplitude** of a sound wave determines its loudness. Loud sound waves have large amplitudes. The larger the sound wave, the more energy is needed to create the wave.

An oscilloscope is useful in studying waves because it gives a picture of the wave that shows the crest and trough of the wave. **Interference** is the interaction of two or more waves that meet. If the waves interfere constructively, the crest of each one meets the crests of the others. They combine into a crest with greater amplitude. As a result, you hear a louder sound. If the waves interfere destructively, then the crest of one meets the trough of another. They produce a wave with lower amplitude that produces a softer sound.

Change in experienced frequency due to relative motion of the source of the sound is called the **Doppler Effect**. When a siren approaches, the pitch is high. When it passes, the pitch drops. As a moving sound source approaches a listener, the sound waves are closer together, causing an increase in frequency in the sound that is heard. As the source passes the listener, the waves spread out and the sound experienced by the listener is lower.

 Electromagnetic Spectrum

Most waves are invisible. Radio waves are used for transmitting data. Common examples are television, cell phones, and wireless computer networks. Microwaves are used to heat food and deliver Wi-Fi service. Infrared waves are utilized in night vision goggles. Visible light is the only range of wavelengths that we can see with our eyes. UV light causes sunburns and would be even more harmful if most of it were not captured in the Earth's ozone layer. X-rays aid us in the medical field and gamma rays are most useful in the field of astronomy.

The electromagnetic spectrum is measured in frequency (f) in hertz and wavelength (λ) in meters. The frequency times the wavelength of every electromagnetic wave equals the speed of light (3.0×10^9 meters/second).

Roughly, the range of wavelengths of the electromagnetic spectrum is:

	f		λ	
Radio waves	10^5 - 10^{-1}	hertz	10^3 - 10^9	meters
Microwaves	10^{-1} - 10^{-3}	hertz	10^9 - 10^{11}	meters
Infrared radiation	10^{-3} - 10^{-6}	hertz	$10^{11.2}$ - $10^{14.3}$	meters
Visible light	$10^{-6.2}$ - $10^{-6.9}$	hertz	$10^{14.3}$ - 10^{15}	meters
Ultraviolet radiation	10^{-7} - 10^{-9}	hertz	10^{15} - $10^{17.2}$	meters
X-Rays	10^{-9} - 10^{-11}	hertz	$10^{17.2}$ - 10^{19}	meters
Gamma Rays	10^{-11} - 10^{-15}	hertz	10^{19} - $10^{23.25}$	meters

Light – Reflection and Refraction

Shadows illustrate one of the basic properties of light. Light travels in a straight line. If you put your hand between a light source and a wall, you will interrupt the light and produce a shadow.

When light hits a surface, it is **reflected**. The angle of the incoming light (angle of incidence) is the same as the angle of the reflected light (angle of reflection). It is this reflected light that allows you to see objects. You see the objects when the reflected light reaches your eyes.

Different surfaces reflect light differently. Rough surfaces scatter light in many different directions. A smooth surface reflects the light in one direction. If it is smooth and shiny (like a mirror) you see your image in the surface.

When light enters a different medium, it bends. This bending, or change of speed, is called **refraction**. For example, if you want to dive for a coin at the bottom of a swimming pool. If you aim directly for the coin, you will miss it. The light rays reflected off the coin are bent as they travel to your eye. Light rays are bent, or refracted, as they pass from water into air. All transparent substances have their own characteristic index of refraction due to the speed of light through that substance.

Light can be **diffracted**, or bent around the edges of an object. Diffraction occurs when light goes through a narrow slit. As light passes through it, the light bends slightly around the edges of the slit. You can demonstrate this by pressing your thumb and forefinger together, making a very thin slit between them. Hold them about 8 cm from your eye and look at a distant source of light. The pattern you observe is caused by the diffraction of light.

Light and other electromagnetic radiation can be polarized because the waves are transverse. The distinguishing characteristic of transverse waves is that they are perpendicular to the direction of the motion of the wave. **Polarized light** has vibrations confined to a single plane that is perpendicular to the direction of motion. Light is able to be polarized by passing it through special filters that block all vibrations except those in a single plane. By blocking out all but one place of vibration, polarized sunglasses cut down on glare.

Light can travel through thin fibers of glass or plastic without escaping the sides. Light on the inside of these fibers is reflected so that it stays inside the fiber until it reaches the other end. Such **fiber optics** are used to carry telephone messages and computer data. Sound waves are converted to electric signals which are coded into a series of light pulses which move through the optical fiber until they reach the other end. At that time, they are converted back into sound.

Mirrors and Lenses

The image that you see in a bathroom mirror appears to be the same distance behind the mirror that you are in front of the mirror. Since it does not really exist, it is a **virtual image** - it only seems to be where it is. However, a curved mirror can produce a **real image**. A real image is produced when light passes through the point where the image appears. A real image can be projected onto a screen.

A **parabolic mirror** is a curved mirror. Parabolic mirrors are used as reflectors for searchlights and automobile headlights. Most shaving mirrors and lighted make-up mirrors are parabolic mirrors. If you look at your face in one, you will see an enlarged image of your face. The surface of a parabolic mirror curves in the shape of a line called a parabola. A line straight out from the center of the mirror is called the **principle axis**. Light rays striking a parabolic mirror parallel to its principle axis are reflected toward a common point in front of the mirror called the **principle focus**. The distance from the center of the mirror to the principle focus is the focal length of the mirror.

Cameras use a convex lens to produce an image on the film. A **convex lens** is thicker in the middle than at the edges. Light is refracted as it passes through a convex lens. The bending of the light rays brings them together at a point called the principal focus. A convex lens is used to form a real image. The image size depends upon the focal length (distance from the focus to the lens). The longer the focal length, the larger the image. A **converging lens** produces a real image whenever the object is far enough from the lens so that the rays of light from the object can hit the lens and be focused into a real image on the other side of the lens.

Eyeglasses can help correct deficiencies of sight by changing where the image seen is focused on the retina of the eye. If a person is **nearsighted**, the lens of his eye focuses images in front of the retina. In this case, the corrective lens placed in the eyeglasses will be concave so that the image will reach the retina. In the case of **farsightedness**, the lens of the eye focuses the images behind the retina. The correction will call for a convex lens to be fitted into the glass frames so that the image is brought forward into sharper focus.

A simple telescope has two convex lenses – the eyepiece lens and the objective lens. A microscope works much in the same way as a telescope.

 Static Electricity

Electrostatics is the study of stationary electric charges. A plastic rod that is rubbed with fur or a glass rod that is rubbed with silk will become electrically charged and will attract small pieces of paper. The charge on the plastic rod rubbed with fur is negative and the charge on glass rod rubbed with silk is positive.

Electrically charged objects share these characteristics:

1. Like charges repel one another.
2. Opposite charges attract each other.
3. Charge is conserved.

A neutral object has no net change. If the plastic rod and fur are initially neutral, when the rod becomes charged by the fur a negative charge is transferred from the fur to the rod. The net negative charge on the rod is equal to the net positive charge on the fur.

All matter is made of atoms which contain equal numbers of negative electrons and positive protons. The electrons can be moved from one atom to another. If electrons are lost, the original atom has a positive charge since it will then have more protons than electrons. If electrons are gained, the atom will have a negative charge since it will then have more electrons than protons. When an object is rubbed it will gain or lose electrons.

In walking across a carpet, your body will pick up an electric charge. If you then touch a metal doorknob, you will feel (and often see) an electric spark. That is the movement of electrons from your hand to the doorknob, called a static discharge.

Materials through which electric charges can easily flow are called **conductors**. Metals (on the left side of the periodic table) are good conductors. On the other hand, an **insulator** is a material through which electric charges do not move easily, if at all. An example of an insulator would be non-metal elements of the periodic table. Rubber and wood are excellent insulators.

A simple device used to indicate the existence of a positive or negative charge is called an **electroscope**. An electroscope is made up of a conducting knob with very light-weight conducting leaves usually made of foil (gold or aluminum). When a charged object touches the knob, the leaves push away from each other because like charges repel. It is not possible to tell whether if the charge is positive or negative.

Charging by induction: Touch the knob with a finger while a charged rod is nearby. The electrons will be repulsed and flow out of the electroscope through the hand. If the hand is removed while the charged rod remains close, the electroscope will retain the charge.

When an object is rubbed with a charged rod, the object will take on the same charge as the rod. However, charging by induction gives the object the opposite charge as that of the charged rod.

Grounding charge: Charge can be removed from an object by connecting it to the earth through a conductor. The removal of static electricity by conduction is called **grounding**.

The French physicist Coulomb found that the force between two charges Q1 and Q2 is directly proportional to the product of the charges and inversely proportional to the square of the distance r between the charges: $F = k Q_1 Q_2 / r^2$. When the charges are in coulombs, the force in newtons, and the distance in meters, the constant k has the value of 8.99×10^9 N-m^2/C^2. This allows us to use the following equation for **Coulomb's Law:**

$$F = (9 \times 10^9 \text{ N-m}^2/\text{C}^2) Q_1 Q_2 / r^2$$

This is directly applicable to charged bodies only in situations in which the distance r between charges is large compared with the dimensions of the charged bodies. When two charged objects are very small compared with the distance between them, we consider them to be point charges.

Any region in which electric forces can be detected is called an **electric field**. The intensity or strength (E) of an electric field at any point is defined as the ratio of the force (F) acting on a small test charge (q) at that point: $E = F/q$. Electric intensity is a vector quantity with its direction being the direction of the force on a positive charge. Lines of force always begin on positive charges and terminate on negative charges.

 Electric Potential

When a small test charge +q is moved about in the field of a fixed charge +Q, work must be done to carry the test charge closer to Q. This work goes into increasing the potential energy of the test charge. On the other hand, as q moves away from Q, the electric field does work, and the potential energy of q decreases. The potential at a point A is the ratio W/q, where W is the work required to move a small test charge +q from infinity to the point A. The unit of potential, the joule (J) per coulomb (C), is called the volt (V).

$$V = W / q = (9 \times 10^9 \text{ V-m/C})Q / r$$

The **potential difference** between two points A and B is simply the potential at A minus the potential at B: $V_{AB} = V_A - V_B$. In other words, the potential difference between two points is one volt if it requires one joule of external work to move one coulomb of charge from one point to the other.

In any electric field the direction of the field is from points at higher potential toward points at lower potential. External work must be supplied to move a positive charge from a point at a lower potential to a point at higher potential.

 Circuits and Electric Current

When two metallic spheres, one charged positively and the other charged negatively, are connected by a copper wire, electrons flow until there is no longer a potential difference between the two spheres. Such a flow of charge is called an **electric current**. The magnitude of the current (I) is the charge per unit of time that passes any cross section of wire: **I = Q / t**. Current flows from a point at higher potential to a point at lower potential as though the current represented a movement of positive charge even though it is the movement of negatively charged electrons.

An **electric circuit** is a path along which electrons flow. A simple circuit can be created with a dry cell, wire, and a device such as a bell or a light bulb. When all are connected, the electrons flow from the negative terminal, through the wire to the device and back to the positive terminal of the dry cell. If there are no breaks in the circuit, the device will work. The circuit is closed. Any break in the flow will create an open circuit and cause the device to shut off.

The device (bell, bulb) is an example of a **load**. A load is a device that uses energy. Suppose that you also add a buzzer so that the bell only rings when you press the buzzer button. The buzzer is acting as a **switch**. A switch is a device that opens or closes a circuit. Pressing the buzzer closes the circuit, making the connection complete and thereby ringing the bell. When the buzzer is not pressed, the circuit is open and the bell is silent.

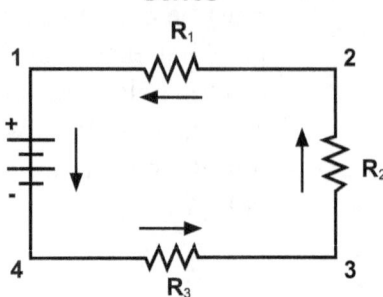

A **series circuit** is one where the electrons have only one path along which they can move. The current is the same through each part. When one load in a series circuit goes out, the circuit is open. An example of this is a set of Christmas tree lights that is missing a bulb. None of the bulbs will work.

A **parallel circuit** is one where the electrons have more than one path to move along. The voltage is the same in each branch. If a load goes out in a parallel circuit, the other load will still work because the electrons can still find a way to continue moving along the path.

When an electron goes through a load, it does work and therefore loses some of its energy. The measure of how much energy is lost is called the **potential difference**. The potential difference between two points is the work needed to move a charge from one point to another. Potential difference is measured in a unit called the volt. The higher the voltage, the more energy the electrons have. This energy is measured by a device called a voltmeter. To use a voltmeter, place it in a circuit parallel with the load you are measuring.

Current, the number of electrons per second that flow past a point in a circuit, is measured with a device called an ammeter. To use an ammeter, put it in series with the load you are measuring.

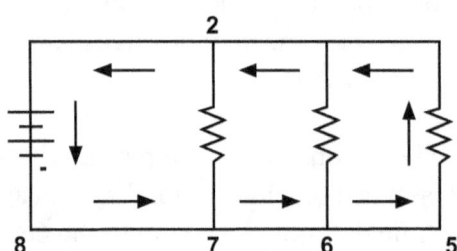

Some the potential energy that is lost by electrons flowing through a wire is changed into heat energy because of resistance. **Resistance** is the ability of the material to oppose the flow of electrons through it. Each substances has a characteristic resistance, even if they are a good conductor such as copper. This resistance is measured in units called **ohms**. A thin wire will have more resistance than a thick one because it will have less room for electrons to travel. In a thicker wire, there will be more possible paths for the electrons to flow. Resistance also depends upon the length of the wire. The longer the wire, the more resistance it will have.

Potential difference, resistance, and current form a relationship known as **Ohm's Law**. Current (I) is measured in amperes and is equal to potential difference (V) measured by volts divided by resistance (R) measured in ohms. **I = V / R**

Example: *If you have a wire with resistance of 5 ohms and a potential difference of 75 volts, what is the current?*

$$I = V / R$$
$$I = 75 \text{ volts} / 5 \text{ ohms} \quad I = 15 \text{ amperes}$$

The power in a circuit is the voltage of the source multiplied by the current produced by the source. Voltage is joules per coulomb. The result of the multiplication is joules per second which is watts.

$$\text{Power (watts)} = \text{voltage (J/C)} \times \text{current (C/s)}$$

P = V I

Therefore, **P = I² R or P = V² / R**
As a result: **W = I² R t**

Example: *A battery has a potential difference of 12 volts. The current produced is 0.33 amperes. What is the power in the circuit?*

$$P = V I$$
$$P = 12 \text{ V} \times 0.33 \text{ A}$$
$$P = 4 \text{ W}$$

 Applied Electricity

The **wiring in a house** is a connected set of simple circuits. For example, the living might contain three ceiling lights, two table lamps, a stereo, and a television. The three ceiling lights are part of a parallel circuit. If one burns out, the others will still work. The switch is wired in series with the lights. All of the lights can be turned on or off at the same time.

The table lamps, stereo, and television plug into wall sockets. Wall sockets are like the terminals of a battery. When you plug a lamp or television into the socket, a circuit is formed. The wall sockets are all parallel. Anything that is plugged in will get the same voltage. The lamp and television are parallel when plugged into the sockets.

The light circuit and wall socket circuit are wired in parallel at the junction box. Here, they are wired in series with a circuit breaker. A circuit breaker is a switch which will open automatically when too much current is being used, overloading the circuit. A current of 10 or more amperes will cause a wire to get hot. 22 amperes is about the maximum for a house circuit. Anything above 25 amperes can start a fire. Circuit breakers in a home monitor the electric current.

Every room circuit in a house is connected to the junction box and a circuit breaker. The main circuit breaker is connected to each individual circuit breaker. After the main circuit breaker, the house is connected to the power line. The main breaker allows us to turn the power on and off. By opening the circuits when too much power is being used, the circuit breakers help prevent electrical fires.

The current in the house is **alternating current**. In alternating current, the electrons rapidly reverse direction repeatedly. The series circuit and parallel circuit shown on the previous page demonstrate **direct current** since the electrons flow only in one direction.

Computers can be made small enough to fit inside a plastic credit card by creating what is known as a solid state device. In this device, electrons flow through solid material such as silicon. A conductor that has a large resistance for its size is called a resistor. Resistors are used to regulate volume on a television or radio or through a dimmer switch for lights.

When caught in an electrical storm, a car is a relatively safe place from lightening because of the resistance of the rubber tires. A metal building would not be safe unless there was a lightening rod that would attract the lightening and conduct it into the ground.

Electric currents are of great practical importance because of the many ways in which we can use the three principal effects they produce: (1) heating, (2) chemical, and (3) magnetic effects. The magnetic effects of currents are used in giant electromagnets and in tiny electric relays in telephone circuits. The interaction between currents and magnetic fields is fundamental to electric motors.

Magnets

Magnets have two poles. The pole (end) which always turns to point toward magnetic north (geographically) is called the north seeking or north pole and the other pole (end) is called the south seeking or south pole. The north poles of two magnets will repel each other, but the north pole of one magnet will attract the south pole of another. Like poles repel and opposite poles attract.

Every magnet exerts a force on other magnets or materials that can be magnetized. A **magnetic field** is the space around a magnet where its force will affect objects. The closer you are to a magnet, the stronger the force. As you move away, the force becomes weaker. The earth has a magnetic field. In a compass, a tiny, lightweight magnet is suspended and will line its south pole up with the North Pole magnet of the earth.

A magnet that holds its magnetic properties over a period of years is a **permanent magnet**. Permanent magnets are made of iron, cobalt, or nickel. Magnets are also made of alloys containing at least one of these metals. A bar magnet and a horseshoe magnet are permanent magnets. A bar magnet has a north pole and a south pole. If you break the magnet in half, each piece will have a north and south pole.

Some materials act as magnets and some do not. This is because magnetism is a result of electrons in motion. The most important motion in this case is the spinning of the individual electrons. Electron pairs spin in opposite directions in most atoms. Each spinning electron has the magnetic field that it creates canceled out by the electron that is spinning in the opposite direction.

In an atom of iron, there are four unpaired electrons. The magnetic fields of these are not canceled out. Their fields add up to make a tiny magnet. There fields exert forces on each other setting up small areas in the iron called **magnetic domains** where atomic magnetic fields line up in the same direction.

You can make a magnet out of an iron nail by stroking the nail in the same direction repeatedly with a magnet. This causes poles in the atomic magnets in the nail to be attracted to the magnet. The tiny magnetic fields in the nail line up in the direction of the magnet. The magnet causes the domains pointing in its direction to grow in the nail. Eventually, one large domain results and the nail becomes a magnet.

Electromagnets

A magnet can be made out of a coil of wire by connecting the ends of the coil to a battery. The current in the wire creates a magnetic field around the wire. Like fields from permanent magnets, fields from electric currents are oriented from north to south. When the current goes through the wire, it is called an **electromagnet**. An electromagnet can be made more powerful in three ways:

1. Make more coils.
2. Put an iron core (nail) inside the coils.
3. Use more battery power.

Air conditioners, vacuum cleaners, and washing machines use electric motors. An electric motor uses an electromagnet to change electric energy into mechanical energy. In a motor, a coil of wire is wound around a shaft. As current passes through the coil, a magnetic field is created in the coil. The effect of the two fields is to turn the shaft because the two opposite fields repel each other.

Another device that uses a coil and a magnet is an **electric meter**. Again the coil is between the poles of a magnet. A needle is attached to the coil. When a current flows through the coil, the coil rotates. The amount of coil rotation depends on the amount of current flowing through it. As the current flowing through the coil increases, the amount of rotation increases. As the coil turns, the needle attached to it shows the amount of rotation. A meter that measures current is called an **ammeter**.

An ammeter and a **voltmeter** have the same basic design. However, the coil in an ammeter has low resistance while the coil in the voltmeter has a very high resistance. When connected to a circuit, very little current flows through its coil. The amount of current that flows through the coil is proportional to the voltage. As the voltage increases, the current in the coil increases.

A **generator** produces electric current by using an electromagnet. When the coil or the magnet rotates, the magnetic field at a point in the wire changes direction. The changing direction of the field changes the direction of the current, creating alternating current.

Half-Cell Potentials

An application of redox, half reactions and net ionic reactions is half-cell potentials in batteries and voltaic cells. The flow of electrons causes reduction at the cathode (negatively charged electrode) and oxidation at the anode (positively charged electrode). A cell must be constructed of two half-cells. The electrical potential of a voltaic cell is the ability of the cell to produce an electric current. The standard cell potential (E^0_{cell}) is the measured cell potential when the ion concentrations in the half-cells are 1.00M, gases are at a pressure of 1 atm, and the temperature is 25° C. Cell potential = $\mathbf{E^0_{cell}}$ = $\mathbf{E^0_{red} - E^0_{oxid}}$ where E^0_{red} is the reduction potential of the half-cell in which reduction occurs and E^0_{oxid} is the reduction potential of the half-cell in which the oxidation occurs.

Example: Ni(s) + Fe^{2+} (aq) → Ni^{2+} (aq) + Fe(s) and
Half cells: Fe^{3+} + e- → Fe^{2+} E^0 Fe^{3+} = + 0.77 V
Ni^{2+} + 2 e- → Ni E^{0}Ni^{2+} = - 0.25 V

Fe^{3+} is reduced and Ni is oxidized. Since reduction takes place at the Fe^{3+} half-cell, this half-cell is the cathode and since oxidation takes place at the Ni half-cell, this half-cell is the anode. Make sure the two half reactions have the same number of electrons. Use a coefficient for one or both of the half-reactions as necessary.

2 (Fe^{3+} + e- → Fe^{2+}) + (Ni^{2+} + 2 e- → Ni) = 2 Fe^{3+} + Ni^{2+} → 2 Fe^{2+} + Ni
Standard cell potential: E$^0_{cell}$ = E$^0_{red}$ - E$^0_{oxid}$
E$^0_{cell}$ = + 0.77 V – (-0.25 V) = + 1.02 V

It is possible to predict if a redox reaction will take place spontaneously using standard reduction potentials. The half-reaction with the more positive reduction potential always undergoes reduction while the half-reaction with the less positive reduction potential undergoes oxidation. If the cell potential for the reaction is positive the reaction is spontaneous. If it is negative, the reverse direction of the reaction is spontaneous (and equally positive).

 Nuclear Chemistry and Radioactivity

Isotopes are called radioisotopes when they have unstable nuclei that are radioactive. **Alpha particles** (α) are positively charged particles (+2) emitted from a radioactive nucleus. They consist of two protons and two neutrons and are identical to the nucleus of a helium atom ($^4_2$He).

Example: $^{238}_{92}$U → $^4_2$He + $^{234}_{90}$Th.

When an atom loses an alpha particle, the Z number (atomic number) is lower by two, so move back two spaces on the periodic table to find what the new element is. The new element has an A number (atomic mass number) that is four less than the original element. Because alpha particles are large and heavy, paper or clothing or even dead skin cells shield from their effects.

There are a number of different types of radioactive decay, the three most common of which are alpha decay, beta decay and gamma decay. When alpha decay occurs, the nucleus spontaneously (i.e. randomly or unpredictably) ejects what is essentially a helium nucleus, or a package of two protons and two neutrons. This results in the atomic number of the atom dropping by two, and the atomic mass dropping by four. Beta decay occurs when the number of neutrons is too high relative to the number of protons. Because the nuclear strong force will not allow an entire neutron to be ejected, the nucleus finds a different solution. When beta decay occurs a neutron is split into a positive and negative portion, becoming a proton and an electron, and the negative portion (i.e., the electron) is ejected. This results in the atomic mass remaining constant, the atomic number increasing by 1 and the charge decreasing by 1. The final type of radiation, gamma radiation, often occurs with other types of radiation when the electrons are left in too high of energy states (or in higher shells than they need to be). The electrons will jump down to the proper shells and emit a gamma ray, which is now known to be a photon (essentially, it just lets out a burst of energy in the form of light).

Beta rays (β) are negatively charged (-1) and fast moving because they are actually electrons. They are written as an electron $^0_{-1}e$ (along with a proton) which is emitted from the nucleus as a neutron decays. Carbon-14 decays by emitting a beta particle.

Example: $^{14}_{6}C \rightarrow {^{14}_{7}N} + {^{0}_{-1}e}$.

The Z number actually adds one since its total must be the same on both the left and the right of the arrow and the electron on the right adds a negative one. The A number is unchanged. The Z determines what the element is, so look for it on the periodic table to determine the product. Metal foil or wood is needed to shield from its effects.

Gamma rays (γ) are high energy electromagnetic waves. They are the same kind of radiation as visible light but of much shorter wavelength and higher frequency. Gamma rays have no mass or charge, so the Z and A numbers are not affected. Radioactive atoms often emit gamma rays along with either alpha or beta particles. Protection from gamma radiation takes lead or concrete.

Example 1: $^{226}_{88}Ra \rightarrow {^{222}_{86}Rn} + {^{4}_{2}He} + \gamma$

Example 2: $^{234}_{90}Th \rightarrow {^{234}_{91}Pa} + {^{0}_{-1}e} + \gamma$

A **positron** is a particle with the mass of an electron but a positive charge ($^0_{+1}e$). It may be emitted as a proton changes to a neutron.

Transmutation is the conversion of an atom of one element to an atom of another element such as occurs in alpha and beta radiation. It also occurs when high-energy particles (such as protons, neutrons, or alpha particles) bombard the nucleus of an atom. The elements in the periodic table with atomic numbers above 92 are called the trans-uranium elements, all of which are radioactive elements that have been synthesized in nuclear reactors and nuclear accelerators.

Example: $^{238}_{92}U + {^{1}_{0}n} \rightarrow {^{239}_{92}U} \rightarrow {^{0}_{-1}e} + {^{239}_{93}Np} \rightarrow {^{239}_{94}Pu} + {^{0}_{-1}e}$

Nuclear fission is the splitting of a nucleus into smaller fragments by bombardment with neutrons. Fission releases enormous amounts of energy. Controlled fission is the source of the energy in nuclear power plants. In **nuclear fusion** hydrogen nuclei fuse to make helium nuclei. Fusion releases even more energy than fission.

Every radioisotope has its own characteristic rate of decay. The **half-life of an isotope** is the time it takes for half the original amount of the isotope in a given sample to decay. For example, the half-life of carbon-14 is 5700 years. If there are 25 grams of carbon-14 in a petrified log, then 5700 years later it will contain 12.5 grams of carbon-14. Another 5700 years later it will contain 6.25 grams of C-14.

CHEMISTRY CONTENT

Atomic Theory and Atomic Structure

An **element** is a substance that can not be broken down into other substances. Elements are assigned an identifying symbol of one or two letters. The symbol for oxygen is O and stands for one atom of oxygen. However, because oxygen atoms in nature are joined together is pairs, the symbol O_2 represents oxygen. This pair of oxygen atoms is a molecule.

An **atom** is the smallest particle of the element that retains the properties of that element. All of the atoms of a particular element are the same. The atoms of each element are different from the atoms of other elements.

The Theory of Atoms was proposed in 1808 by John Dalton:

1. Each element is made up of tiny particles called atoms.
2. The atoms of a given element are identical; the atoms of different elements are different in some fundamental way or ways.
3. Chemical compounds are formed when atoms combine with each other. A given compound always has the same relative numbers and types of atoms.
4. Chemical reactions involve reorganization of the atoms – changes in the way they are bound together. The atoms themselves are not changed in a chemical reaction.

Atoms are composed of **protons** and **neutrons** in the nucleus, providing the mass of the atom. Protons are positively charged particles and neutrons are neutral. Early work in electricity helped with the discovery of **electrons**, negatively charged particles with 2000 times less mass than hydrogen and 1840 times less mass than either protons or neutrons. (Each proton and neutron is composed of three quarks.) The electrons surround the nucleus in a sort of cloud.

The **atomic number** of an element is the number of protons it has. In an atom, the number of electrons equals the number of protons so that the atom has no charge. Its **mass number** is the actual number of protons plus neutrons in the nucleus. For example, hydrogen (H) has the atomic number 1 because its nucleus contains only one proton. The number of neutrons in a nucleus varies, sometimes being equal to the number of protons and sometimes being more or less. This results in elements which have an atomic mass (the sum of the masses of protons and neutrons) which varies from atom to atom. Atoms with the same number of protons but different numbers of electrons are referred to as isotopes. For example, Carbon-12, Carbon-13 and Carbon-14 are the most common isotopes of the element carbon, having an atomic mass of 12, 13, and 14 respectively. The atomic number of carbon is 6. Therefore the three isotopes have 6, 7, and 8 neutrons respectively.

Another characteristic of atoms is that they will bond with other atoms. The factor which determines whether an element will bond, what type of bond it will form, and which other elements it will bond with is the number of electrons. Electrons exist around the nucleus in shells. The first shell holds two electrons, and all shells beyond that hold eight. The outermost shell which an atom has electrons is in referred to as the valence shell, and the atoms in that shell are the valence electrons. Atoms will form bonds so that their outer shells are as full as possible. For example, nitrogen, with atomic number 7, has 7 electrons and therefore 5 valence electrons. This means that it will typically bond in ways to gain three additional electrons. On the other hand, neon, with atomic number 10, has a full valence shell. Because of this it is difficult to get neon to bond and react with other elements.

Isotopes are atoms of the same element so they have the same number of protons, but they have different numbers of neutrons. Most elements occur as two or more isotopes in nature. A mass spectrometer is used to separate atoms of slightly different masses, so it can separate the isotopes of samples of naturally occurring elements which are mixtures of isotopes.

The **atomic mass** (also known as **atomic weight**) of an element is the weighted average of the masses of the isotopes of that element. Therefore, if 92.0% of the atoms of an element have a mass of 28.0 amu, 6.0% have a mass of 29.0 amu, and the rest (2.0%) have a mass of 30.0 amu, the average atomic mass is (0.92)(28.0 amu) + (0.06)(29.0 amu) + (0.02)(30.0 amu) = 25.76 amu + 1.74 amu + 0.60 amu = 28.1 amu which makes it silicon. An **atomic mass unit** (amu) is defined as one-twelfth of the mass of a carbon atom that contains six protons and six neutrons.

As the masses of the elements were found, the elements were placed on a table to try to organize them. The **Periodic Table of the Elements** used today is based on the one created by Dmitri Mendeleev who saw that many of the elements were metals and that most of the elements could be grouped according to various properties. Each box in the table shows at least four pieces of data: (1) the element symbol represented by one or two letters, the first letter is capitalized with the second one being lower case, (2) the element name, (3) the atomic number, and (4) the atomic weight. The elements are arranged in the periodic table in vertical columns called groups or families which have similar chemical properties and in horizontal rows called periods which are based on their electron configurations. When Mendeleev's table appeared, there were blank spots where properties of an element were predicted but the element had not been discovered. Elements discovered after his table fit those blanks.

Electrons determine the chemical behavior of an element. Each electron in an atom can be described by a unique set of four quantum numbers, n, l, m and s. The principal quantum number (n = 1, 2, 3, ...) is the number of the energy level (sometimes called the electron shell number) and describes the relative electron cloud size (how many electrons and what level and sublevel). The seven principal quantum numbers correspond to the seven periods (rows) on the periodic table. Each energy level has sublevels (s, p, d, and f) of the principal quantum number.

The second quantum number (l = 0, 1, 2, ... which is n – 1) describes the shape of the cloud. The third quantum number, m, describes the orientation in space of each orbital. Each orbital may contain a maximum of one pair of electrons. Electrons in the same orbital have opposite spins. Accordingly, the fourth quantum number (s = + ½ or – ½) describes the spin direction of the electron. Pauli's exclusion principle states that no two electrons in an atom can have the same set of quantum numbers.

The s subshell has one orbital which can have up to two electrons, the p subshell which can have up to three orbitals with six electrons, the d subshell has five orbitals which can have up to ten electrons, and the f subshell has seven orbitals which can have up to fourteen electrons. Subshells fill in the order in which the arrows are shown:

$1s^2$			
$2s^2$	$2p^6$		
$3s^2$	$3p^6$	$3d^{10}$	
$4s^2$	$4p^6$	$4d^{10}$	$4f^{14}$
$5s^2$	$5p^6$	$5d^{10}$	$5f^{14}$
$6s^2$	$6p^6$	$6d^{10}$	
$7s^2$	$7p^6$		

For example: Hydrogen is $1s^1$ and Helium is $1s^2$. Oxygen has an atomic number of eight, so it has eight electrons or $1s^2\ 2s^2\ 2p^4$. Iodine with 53 electrons could be notated as $1s^2\ 2s^2\ 2p^6\ 3s^2\ 3p^6\ 4s^2\ 3d^{10}\ 4p^6\ 5s^2\ 4d^{10}\ 5p^5$ or as (Kr) $5s^2\ 4d^{10}\ 5p^5$ using the configuration of the closest previous noble gas. Since the electrons fill the orbitals with opposite spins, the total electron configuration for Fluorine would be:

$1s^2$	$2s^2$	$2p^5$
X	X	X X \

Spin directions, shown by the two crosses of the X, are sometimes shown by an "up" arrow and a "down" arrow (↑ ↓). Electrons with the lowest energy are in orbitals closest to the nucleus with each energy level out from the nucleus taking more energy to attain. Electrons normally occupy the set of orbitals that give the atom the lowest overall energy.

Periodic Properties

Noble gases have the most stable outer electron configurations. They are the least reactive of the elements. These "inert" gases are Group 8A because they have eight electrons (s^2p^6) in their outermost energy level.

The elements of Period 1A all (except Hydrogen) have one electron in their outermost energy level so they have an s1 configuration. Therefore, they have one **valence electron** and, when they give that electron up to become an ion, they have a charge of +1. Positive ions are called **cations**. In general, elements with three or fewer electrons in their outermost energy level (at left, in aqua) are considered to be metals and lose their electrons to become cations.

The elements of Period 7A all (except Helium) have seven electrons in their outermost energy level so they have s^2p^5 configuration. Therefore, they have seven valence electrons, so they desire to add an electron to become an ion. That makes them **anions** (negative ions) with a charge of -1. Generally, elements with five or more electrons in their outermost energy level (at right, in salmon) are considered nonmetals and are likely to gain electrons to become anions.

The B elements are transition elements and most have two electrons in their outermost energy level. Metalloids, those elements along the heavy stair-step line, show properties of both metals and nonmetals. The two series below the main periodic table are called Lanthanoids (upper) and Actinoids (lower).

Key Facts about the Elements

Group	Name	Configuration	Charges	Properties
1A	Alkali metals	s^1	+1	Reactive, hard, shiny, conduct heat & electricity, malleable, ductile, ionic, solid
2A	Alkaline earth metals	s^2	+2	Reactive, hard, shiny, conduct heat & electricity, malleable, ductile, ionic, solid
3A	Aluminum group	s^2p^1	+3	
4A	Carbon group	s^2p^2	+4 or -4	Covalent
5A	N & P group	s^2p^3	-3	
6A	Chalcogens	s^2p^4	-2	
7A	Halogens	s^2p^5	-1	Reactive, ionic, gas
8A	Noble gases	s^2p^6	0	Nonreactive, gas

Periodic Properties:

1. **Atomic Radius** (size) – the radius of the atom measured from the center of the nucleus to the outermost electron or, if it is a covalent atomic radius it is measured as half the distance between the nuclei of two atoms of the diatomic molecule
2. **Electron Affinity** – energy change accompanying the addition of an electron to an atom to make a negative ion (anion)
3. **Ionic Size** – the radius of an ion measured from the center of the nucleus to the outermost electron. Going left to right there is a gradual decrease through the positive ions as they lose electrons and therefore an energy level, but Group 5 is much bigger due to keeping the energy level and gaining an electron and then there is a slight decrease going through Group 7.
4. **Electronegativity** – tendency for an atom to attract electrons to itself in bonding
5. **Shielding Effect** – a decrease in attraction between an atom's nucleus and its outer electrons due to the electrons between the nucleus and the outer electrons
6. **Ionization Energy** – energy necessary to remove an electron from an atom to make an ion. Factors affecting ionization energy:
    a. Nuclear charge – the larger the nuclear charge, the greater the IE
    b. Shielding effect – the greater the shielding effect, the less the IE
    c. Radius – the greater the distance between the nucleus and the outer electrons of an atom, the less the IE
    d. Sublevel – an electron from a sublevel that is more than half-full requires additional energy to be removed

Summary of periodic trends on the Periodic Table*:

*Note: Memorize the ones in italics; everything else increases top→bottom, left→right

Group Trends (top to bottom):
Increases: atomic radius, nuclear charge, ionic size, shielding effect, atomic number (number of protons, number of electrons)
Decreases: ionization energy, electron affinity, electronegativity

Period Trends (left to right):
Increases: electronegativity, nuclear charge, ionization energy, electron affinity, atomic number (number of protons, number of electrons)
Decreases all the way across: atomic radius
Decreases through cations (positive) and again through anions: ionic size Stays the same left to right: shielding effect

Physical properties and chemical properties of matter describe the appearance or behavior of a substance. A **physical property** can be observed without changing the identity of a substance. For instance, you can describe the color, mass, shape, and volume of a book. **Chemical properties** describe the ability of a substance to be changed into new substances. Baking powder goes through a chemical change as it changes into carbon dioxide gas during the baking process.

A calculated physical property based on two other physical properties is density. **Density** (D) is the mass (m) of a substance contained per unit of volume (V), or D = m/V. Density is stated in grams per cubic centimeter (g/cm^3). If the density of an object is less than the density of a liquid, the object will float in the liquid. If the object is denser than the liquid, then the object will sink.

Matter constantly changes. A **physical change** is a change that does not produce a new substance. The freezing and melting of water is an example of physical change. A **chemical change** (or chemical reaction) is any change of a substance into one or more other substances. Burning materials turn into smoke; a seltzer tablet fizzes into gas bubbles.

Atomic Models of the Atom

The present model of the atom is much different from Dalton's model. In the late 1800's, a British scientist named **J. J. Thompson** was studying how electric current flowed through a vacuum tube. His hypothesis was that if rays are made of charged particles, then an electric field would attract them. Further, if it is a charged particle, then a magnet will affect its motion. From his work, Thompson proved that the rays were made of negative particles. These particles were later called electrons. The results of his experimentation produced **Thompson's Model is often referred to as the plum pudding model:** The atom is made of negative particles equally mixed in a sphere of positive material.

Ernest Rutherford studied atomic structure in 1910-1911 by firing a beam of alpha particles at thin layers of gold leaf. According to Thomson's model, the path of an alpha particle should be deflected only slightly if it struck an atom, but Rutherford observed some alpha particles bouncing almost backwards, suggesting that nearly all the mass of an atom is contained in a small positively charged nucleus. Rutherford's model of the atom was an analogy to the **sun and the planets**. A small positively charged nucleus is surrounded by circling negatively charged electrons and empty space.

The Danish scientist **Neils Bohr** created a model in 1913. The results of his model are:

1. Electrons orbit the nucleus, but as long as the electron stays in an "allowed orbit" it will not lose energy.

2. When an electron moves from an outer orbit to an inner orbit, it gives off energy.

3. When an electron moves from an inner orbit to an outer orbit, it absorbs energy.

Bohr's model only explains the very simplest atoms, such as hydrogen. Today's more sophisticated atomic model is based upon how waves react. **Louis de Broglie's model of the atom** described electrons as **matter waves in standing wave orbits** around the nucleus.

The realization that both matter and radiation interact as waves led **Werner Heisenberg** to the conclusion in 1927 that there is an inherent limitation in the ability to measure phenomena at the subatomic level. This is known as the **Heisenberg uncertainty principle**, and it applies to the location and momentum of electrons in an atom.

When **Erwin Schrödinger** studied the atom in 1925, he replaced the idea of precise orbits with regions in space called **orbitals** where electrons were likely to be found. **The Schrödinger equation** describes the **probability** that an electron will be in a given region of space, a quantity known as electron density.

Wolfgang Pauli helped develop quantum mechanics in the 1920s by developing the concept of spin and the **Pauli exclusion principle**, which states that if two electrons occupy the same orbital, they must have different spin (intrinsic angular momentum).

Friedrich Hund determined a set of rules to determine the ground state of a multi-electron atom in the 1920s. One of these rules is called **Hund's Rule** in introductory chemistry courses, and describes the order in which electrons fill orbitals and their spin.

Chemical Bonding

The primary types of bonding between or among atoms are ionic and covalent. Other types of bonding are hydrogen, metallic, van der Waals, and macromolecular. Atoms are most stable with eight electrons in their outermost energy level, so atoms will either gain or lose electrons to attain that configuration (octet rule).

Ionic and Metallic Bonding

Ions are atoms or groups of atoms with a positive or negative charge. The chart "key facts about elements" shows the charges on elemental ions and the paragraphs prior to the chart explain those charges. The ionization energies for electrons of elements with fewer than four in their outermost energy level are quite low, so it is relatively easy to draw those electrons away to satisfy the octet rule. The charge of cations equals the number of electrons lost and positive since they now have more protons (positive) than electrons (negative).

The electron affinities for elements on the right side of the periodic table are quite low which allows them to attract atoms to satisfy the octet rule. The charge of anions equals the number of electrons gained and negative since they now have more electrons (negative) than protons (positive).

Positive ions (cations) electrostatically attract negative ions (anions) to create an ionic compound through ionic bonding. The total positive charge equals the total negative charge, giving the compound a charge of zero. Nearly all ionic compounds are crystalline solids at room temperature. The ions form a specific and predictable shape of crystal by their orderly arrangement. A coordination number indicates the number of ions of opposite charge that surround each ion in a crystal.

Bond angles, total number of electron pairs, number of shared pairs, and number of unshared pairs determine the shape of a crystal. There are five basic shapes: linear (3 atoms), trigonal planar (4 atoms), tetrahedral (5 atoms), trigonal bipyramidal (6 atoms), and octahedral (7 atoms). The basic shapes have no unshared pairs of electrons. When there is an unshared pair of electrons, the shape and bond angles remain about the same but there is a blank spot where there had been a shared pair of electrons.

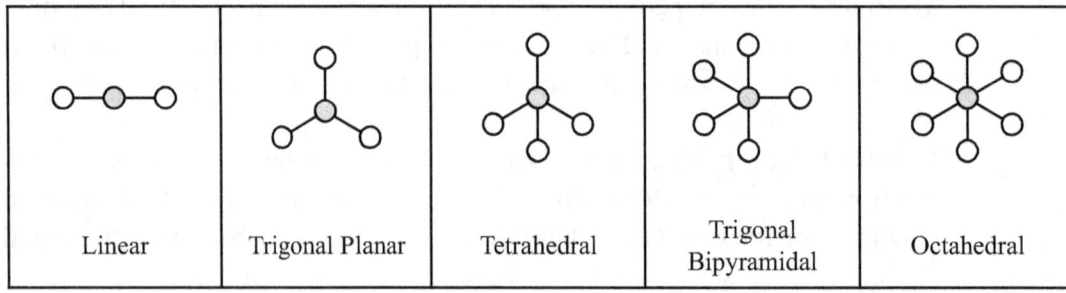

| Linear | Trigonal Planar | Tetrahedral | Trigonal Bipyramidal | Octahedral |

Molecules with three atoms can be linear (no unshared pairs of electrons or three unshared pairs of electrons (a variation of trigonal bipyramidal), or bent which is a variation of trigonal planar (1 unshared pair) or tetrahedral (2 unshared pairs). With four atoms, the shape can be trigonal planar (0 unshared pairs), or trigonal pyramidal (1 unshared pair) which is a variation of tetrahedral or T-shaped planar (2 unshared pairs) which is a variation of trigonal bipyramidal. A molecule of five atoms can have the shape of tetrahedral (0 unshared pairs) or irregular tetrahedron (1 unshared pair, a variation of trigonal bipyramidal), or square planar (2 unshared pairs, a variation of octahedral). With six atoms, the possible shapes are trigonal bipyramidal (0 unshared pairs) or square pyramidal (1 unshared pair, a variation of octahedral). Octahedral is the main choice for seven atoms.

Sample Molecule	Number of Atoms	Electron Pair Geometry	Total Number of Electron Pairs	Number of Shared Pairs	Number of Unshared Pairs	Molecular Shape
BeF_2	3	sp	2	2	0	Linear
GaF_3	4	sp^2	3	3	0	Trigonal planar
O_3	3	sp^2	3	2	1	Bent
CH_4	5	sp^3	4	4	0	Tetrahedral
NH_3	4	sp^3	4	3	1	Trigonal pyramidal
H_2O	3	sp^3	4	2	2	Bent
$NbBr_5$	6	sp^3d	5	5	0	Trigonal bipyramidal
SF_4	5	sp^3d	5	4	1	Irregular tetrahedron
BrF_3	4	sp^3d	5	3	2	T-shaped Planar
XeF_2	3	sp^3d	5	2	3	Linear
SF_6	7	sp^3d^2	6	6	0	Octahedral
IF_5	6	sp^3d^2	6	5	1	Square pyramid
XeF_4	5	sp^3d^2	6	4	2	Square planar

Polyatomic ions are groups of atoms that behave as a unit and carry a charge just as an ion does and they combine with ions to form ionic compounds. Use the chart below to memorize the "-ate" ions; then remember (1) that "per_ate" means one more oxygen than "ate" but the same charge, (2) that "-ite" means one less oxygen than "-ate" but the same charge, and (3) that "hypo_ite" means one less oxygen than "-ite" but the same charge.

Polyatomic Ions and Their Charges

Charge	Ions	Names
-3	PO_4	Phosphate
-2	O_2	Peroxide
	SO_4	Sulfate
	CO_3	Carbonate
	CrO_4	Chromate
	Cr_2O_7	Dichromate
-1	OH	Hydroxide
	ClO_3	Chlorate
	MnO_4	Permanganate
	CN	Cyanide
+1	H	Hydrogen
	NH_4	Ammonium
	Metal(I)	All metals with a Roman numeral I (-ous)
+2	Metal(II)	All metals with a Roman numeral II
+3	Metal(III)	All metals with a Roman numeral III
+4	Metal(IV)	All metals with a Roman numeral IV
+5	Metal(V)	All metals with a Roman numeral V

Metals are like ionic compounds in some ways. They consist of positive metal ions packed together and surrounded by a sea of their valence electrons to create the metallic bond. The valence electrons are free to travel from one end of a piece of metal to the other, accounting for the excellent electrical conductivity, malleability, and ductility. Metals are simple crystalline solids, usually in one of three basic shapes – body-centered cubic, face-centered cubic, or hexagonal close-packed arrangement.

 Covalent Bonding

Covalent bonding is the **sharing of electrons** to acquire a stable electron configuration to create a **molecular compound**. A shared pair of electrons forms a **single covalent bond**. If two or three pairs of electrons are shared, double or triple bonds are formed. When only one of the atoms in a bond provides the pair of bonding electrons, it is a **coordinate covalent bond**. Molecular compounds tend to have relatively low melting and boiling points and often exist as gases or liquids at room temperature and may be composed of two or more nonmetallic elements (example: CO_2). Organic compounds are covalently bonded (see section on organic chemistry).

If the bonding electrons are shared equally, the bond is nonpolar. However, if the bonding electrons are shared unequally, the bond is polar and the amount of polarity is determined by consulting a table of electronegativities. If the electronegativity difference is less than 0.4 the bond is nonpolar covalent, if it is a 0.4 to 1.0 difference the bond is moderately polar covalent, and if it is 1.0-2 the bond is very polar covalent. (An electronegativity difference greater than 2.0 indicates an ionic bond.) In a **polar molecule** one end has negative character and the other end has positive character, creating a dipole. The shape of the molecule as well as the polarity of each bond affects the polarity of the whole molecule.

Just as there are atomic orbitals (s, p, d, f), there are **molecular orbitals** produced when two atoms combine and their orbitals overlap. The overlap of two atomic orbitals produces two molecular orbitals, one of which is a bonding orbital and the other is an antibonding orbital. The bonding orbital has a lower energy than the atomic orbitals from which it is formed and the antibonding orbital has a higher energy than that of either of the atomic orbitals from which it is formed.

Intermolecular Attractions

A great variety of physical properties occurs among covalent compounds due to **intermolecular attractions**, those attractions that occur between molecules. They are responsible for whether the molecular compound is a gas, a liquid, or a solid. They are weaker than either ionic or covalent bonding though. The weakest forces are called **van der Waals forces** and include dispersion forces and dipole interactions. **Dispersion forces** are caused by the motion of electrons. Molecules with few electrons such as fluorine tend to be gases due to weak dispersion force attraction while molecules with more electrons like bromine tend to be liquids and those with even more attraction due to more electrons tend to be solids at room temperature. **Dipole interactions** are a type of electrostatic attraction between polar molecules. Because the hydrogens in water have a slightly positive charge and the oxygen has a slightly negative charge, the hydrogens in one molecule are attracted to oxygens in other molecules. This attraction pulls the molecules closer together and contributes to the spherical drop of water.

A **hydrogen bond** is a weak, secondary bond between a partially positive hydrogen atom and a partially negative (highly electronegative) N, O, or F atom in the same molecule or a nearby molecule. Hydrogen bonds are the strongest of the intermolecular forces. The properties of water and biological molecules like proteins are greatly determined by hydrogen bonds.

Network solids are substances in which all the atoms are covalently bonded to each other. Diamond, made entirely of carbon, is a network solid because each carbon is covalently bonded to four other carbons. Network solids have very high melting points.

Compounds

Substances can combine without a chemical change. A **mixture** is any combination of two or more substances in which the substances keep their own properties. A fruit salad is a mixture. Colognes and perfumes are the other examples. You may not readily recognize the individual elements. However, they can be separated.

Compounds and **mixtures** are similar in that they are made up of two or more substances. However, they have the following opposite characteristics:

Compounds:
1. Made up of one kind of particle
2. Formed during a chemical change
3. Broken down only by chemical changes
4. Properties are different from its parts
5. Has a specific amount of each ingredient

Mixtures:
1. Made up of two or more particles
2. Not formed by a chemical change
3. Can be separated by physical changes
4. Properties are the same as its parts
5. Does not have a definite amount of each ingredient

A compound is a pure substance formed from the combination of two or more elements that differs from the elements in it. Compounds obey the **law of definite proportions** which says that the elements in a compound always combine in the same proportion by mass. All compounds are electrically neutral. There are two types of compounds: **ionic compounds** are formed using ions and use electrostatic charge and attraction while **molecular compounds** are formed of covalently bonded atoms. The smallest unit of either one is sometimes referred to as a **molecule**; however, the molecule is the smallest unit of a molecular compound while a **formula unit** is the smallest unit of an ionic compound.

Summary of Characteristics of Ionic and Covalent Compounds

Characteristic	Ionic Compound	Covalent Compound
Representative unit	Formula unit	Molecule
Bond Formation	Transfer of one or more electrons between atoms	Sharing of electron pairs between atoms
Physical State	Solid	Solid, Liquid, or Gas
Type of Elements	Metallic and nonmetallic	Nonmetallic
Melting Point	High	Low
Solubility in Water	High	High to Low
Electrical conductivity	Good	Poor

The composition of each compound is represented by a **chemical formula** which shows the kinds and numbers of atoms in a formula unit of an ionic compound or a **molecular formula** which shows the number and kinds of atoms present in a molecule of a molecular compound. The **law of multiple proportions** states that whenever two elements form more than one compound, the different masses of one element that combine with the same mass of the other element are in the ratio of small whole numbers.

Naming Compounds

<u>Naming Binary Ionic Compounds in which the cation has only one valence</u> (such as 1A, 2A, and aluminum):
1. The cation is named first, the anion second.
2. A monatomic cation takes its name from the name of the element.
3. A monatomic anion is named by taking the first part of the element name and adding –ide.
4. Examples: sodium chloride is NaCl, lithium nitride is Li_3N

<u>Naming Binary Ionic Compounds in which the cation has more than one valence</u> (such as transition ions):
1. The charge on the metal ion must be specified, such as iron(II) and iron(III) denoting Fe+2 and Fe+3 respectively. In an older method, the ion with the lower charge has a name ending in –ous (Ferrous = Fe+2) and the ion with the higher charge has a name ending in –ic (Ferric = Fe+3).
2. The cation is named first, the anion second.
3. A monatomic anion is named by taking the first part of the element name and adding –ide.
4. Examples: iron(III) oxide (ferric oxide) is Fe_2O_3, tin(IV) chloride is $SnCl_4$

Naming Binary Covalent Compounds (between two nonmetals):
1. The first element in the formula is named first using the full element name.
2. The second element is named as if it were an anion.
3. Prefixes are used to denote the numbers of atoms present. These prefixes are di- for two, tri- for three, tetra- for four, penta- for five, etc. No prefix is needed for a single atom which is the first element named.
4. Examples: silicon tetrabromide is $SiBr_4$, dinitrogen monoxide is N_2O

Naming Acids:
1. Normally the cation in acids is H+ and the compounds are dissolved in water or give water as a product. Most of these compounds can be named two ways.
2. When the anion ends in –ide, the acid name begins with the prefix hydro- such that HC_1 is hydrogen chloride or hydrochloric acid and H_2S is hydrogen sulfide or hydrosulfuric acid.
3. Polyatomic ions ending in –ate become –ic acids such that HC_1O_3 is hydrogen chlorate or chloric acid and HC_1O_4 is hydrogen perchlorate or perchloric acid.
4. Polyatomic ions ending in –ite become –ous acids such that HC_1O_2 is hydrogen chlorite or chlorous acid and HC_1O is hydrogen hypochlorite or hypochlorous acid.

The Mole Concept

The term representative particle refers to the smallest unit of a substance which can be an atom, an ion, or a molecule. Normally the representative particle of an element is an atom. Seven elements do not exist as single atoms in nature, but as diatomic molecules. They are easy to remember using a rule of 7's: there are seven of them, they make a 7 on the Periodic Table, and most are in Period 7A – nitrogen (N_2), oxygen (O_2), fluorine (F_2), chlorine (Cl_2), bromine (Br_2), iodine (I_2) plus hydrogen (H2).

In 1809 Joseph Gay-Lussac found that two volumes of hydrogen reacted with one volume of oxygen (at the same temperature and pressure) to form two volumes of water and that one volume of hydrogen reacted with one volume of chlorine to form two volumes of hydrogen chloride. In 1811 Amadeo Avogadro's hypothesis interpreted Joseph Gay-Lussac's work: Equal volumes of different gases at the same temperature and pressure contain the same number of particles. Under these conditions the volume of a gas is determined by the number of molecules present. Thus,

$$2\ H_2 + O_2 \rightarrow 2\ H_2O \text{ and } 2\ H_2 + Cl_2 \rightarrow 2\ HC_1$$

The number of particles in one "volume" of hydrogen is the same as the number of particles in one "volume" of any other element just as the number of eggs in a dozen is always twelve. That number of particles, the **mole**, is named **Avogadro's number** and is equal to **6.02×10^{23}**. For example, one mole of magnesium is 6.02×10^{23} atoms of magnesium and one mole of oxygen is 6.02×10^{23} molecules, but since each molecule has two atoms it is (2 atoms/molecule)(6.02×10^{23} molecules) or 1.204×10^{24} atoms. Notice that in (atoms/~~molecule~~)(~~molecule~~) the molecules cancel each other.

The **gram atomic mass** is the number of grams of an element that is numerically equal to the atomic mass in amu. For hydrogen, the gram atomic mass is 1 amu just as the gram atomic mass of carbon is 12 amu (its atomic weight). The mass of one mole of a compound is its **gram formula mass** which is the total of the gram atomic masses multiplied by their subscripts in the formula of the elements.

> Example: *Calculate the gram formula mass of $Al_2(SO_4)_3$ aluminum sulfate:*
>
> The subscript of 2 next to Al means there are two moles of aluminum, so aluminum's atomic mass must be multiplied by two.
>
> The subscript of 4 with the O means there are four moles of oxygen in sulfate, so the atomic mass of oxygen must be multiplied by four.
>
> The subscript of 3 with the SO_4 means there are three moles of sulfate. In this case, sulfur's atomic mass must be multiplied by three and oxygen's must be multiplied by 3 x 4 (above) or 12.
>
> For Al: 2 moles x 28.98 g/mole = 57.96 g
> For O: 12 moles x 16.00 g/mole = 152.00 g
> For S: 3 moles x 32.06 g/mole = 96.18 g
> Total of Gram Formula Mass = 57.96 g + 152.00 g + 96.18 g = 306.14 g

The term **molar mass** can be used in place of gram formula mass to refer to the mass of a mole of atoms or molecules or formula units of any element or compound.

Conversions between moles and grams of a substance are done using the gram formula mass such that **moles of substance x gram formula mass = grams of substance.** Using this formula, moles x grams/mole allows moles to cancel and leaves you with grams. If the number of grams is known, flip the gram formula mass upside down (1 mole of carbon = 12 grams or 12 grams of carbon = 1 mole can be expressed and used as 1 mole C / 12 g C or 12 g C / 1 mole C) and multiply by the mass to cancel grams and get moles.

Example 1: *Find the mass in grams of 5.0 mol H_2O_2.* The gram formula mass of H_2O_2 is 2(1 g H/mol H) + 2(16 g O/mol O) = 2 g + 32 g = 34 g/mol H_2O_2.
5.0 mol H_2O_2 x 34 g H_2O_2 / 1 mol H_2O_2 = 170 grams H_2O_2

Example 2: Find the number of moles in 333 g SnF_2. The gram formula mass of SnF_2 is 1(118.69 g Sn/mol Sn) + 2(18.00 g F_2/mol F_2) = 118.69 g + 36 g = 154.69 g/mol SnF_2.
333 g SnF_2 x 1 mol SnF_2 / 154.69 g SnF_2 = 2.15 mol SnF_2

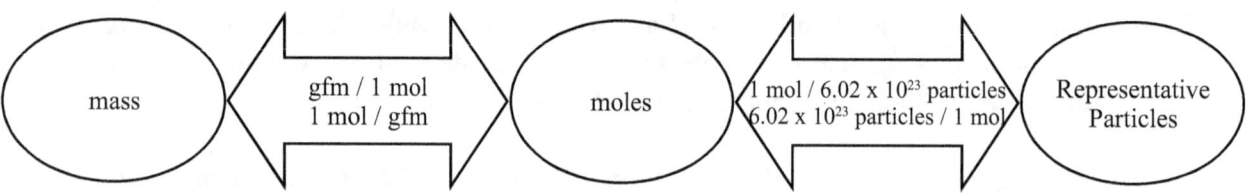

PERCENT COMPOSITION AND EMPIRICAL FORMULA

Percent composition is the percent by mass of each element in a compound. It includes as many percents there are elements in the compound.

Example: *Calculate the percent composition of the compound formed from 222.6 g of Na and 77.4 g of O.* Add the two masses to find the total mass of the compound:

$$222.6 + 77.4 \text{ g} = 300.0 \text{ g}$$

% element = mass element / mass of compound x 100 %
% Na = mass Na / mass of cmpd x 100 % = 222.6 g Na / 300.0 g Na_xO_x = 74.2 % Na
% O = 77.4 g O / 300 g a_xO_x x 100 % = 25.8 % O

The two percentages have to add up to 100%: 74.2% + 25.8% = 100%

To calculate the percent by mass of an element in a known compound, divide the mass of the element in one mole by the gram formula mass of the compound and multiply by 100%.

Percent composition can be used to calculate the number of grams of an element in a specific amount of a compound.

Example: *Using the percent composition, calculate the amount of hydrogen in 378 g HCN.* Use the subscripts as the number of moles, so H = 1, C = 1, and N = 1.

$$(1 \text{ mol H}) (1 \text{ g H} / 1 \text{ mol H}) = 1 \text{ g H}$$
$$(1 \text{ mol C}) (12 \text{ g C} / 1 \text{ mol C}) = 12 \text{ g C}$$
$$(1 \text{ mol N}) (14 \text{ g N} / 1 \text{ mol N}) = 14 \text{ g N}$$
Gram formula mass (gfm) of HCN = 1 g + 12 g + 14 g = 27 g HCN
$$\% \text{ H} = 1 \text{ g H} / 27 \text{ g HCN} \times 100\% = 3.7 \% \text{ H}$$
$$\% \text{ C} = 12 \text{ g C} / 27 \text{ g HCN} \times 100\% = 44.4 \% \text{ C}$$
$$\% \text{ N} = 14 \text{ g N} / 27 \text{ g HCN} \times 100\% = 51.9 \% \text{ N}$$
Check: 3.7 % + 44.4 % + 51.9 % = 100.0 %
grams H = (3.7 %)(1 / 100%)(378 g H) = 14.0 g H

An **empirical formula** is the formula with the lowest whole-number ratio of elements in a compound such that the empirical formula for hydrogen peroxide (H_2O_2) is HO.

Example: *Calculate the empirical formula of a compound that is 79.8% C and 20.2% H.*
Assume 100 grams of the compound. Therefore, 79.8 g are C and 20.2 g are H. Use gram formula mass to convert to moles. (79.8 g C)(1 mol C / 12 g C) = 6.65 mol C and (20.2 g H)(1 mol H / 1 g H) = 20.2 mol H. This does not give a whole number ratio – 6.65:20.2 so divide 20.2 by 6.65 to get 3.04 which is pretty close to the whole number 3. That means that there are 3 H for every C, so the empirical formula is CH_3.

The molecular formula of a compound can be determined from its empirical formula and its gram formula mass. Once the empirical formula is found, calculate its mass. Then divide the known gram formula mass by the empirical mass to find what number to use to multiply all the subscripts of the empirical formula.

Example: *Determine the molecular formula for a compound that is 94.1 % O and 5.9 % H and has a gram formula mass of 34 grams.*

$$(0.941 \text{ g O})(1 \text{ mol O} / 16 \text{ g O}) = 0.059 \text{ mol O}$$
$$(0.059 \text{ g H})(1 \text{ mol H} / 1 \text{ g H}) = 0.059 \text{ mol H}$$
Since this is a 1:1 ratio, the empirical formula is HO.
The empirical mass = 1 g H + 16 g O = 17 g HO.
The gram formula mass is 34 grams; therefore, 34 grams / 17 grams = 2.
Multiply the subscripts (of 1) by 2 to get a molecular formula of H_2O_2

Liquids and Solids

Since the particles of both **liquids** and gases are in constant motion and are free to slide past each other, they can flow and are referred to as fluids. However, the particles of liquids are held together by weak attractive forces which must be overcome for those particles to escape the liquid. These forces also reduce the space between particles. Vapor pressure, heat of vaporization, and boiling point of a liquid are determined by the interplay of the motion of the particles, heat, and pressure.

Vaporization is the conversion of a liquid to a gas (or vapor). It is the escape of molecules from the surface of the liquid. Only those molecules which possess enough kinetic energy can escape the bonds at the surface. Some that escape collide with air molecules and fall back into the liquid, called **condensation**. The liquid **evaporates** (becomes vapor) faster when heated.

Vapor pressure is created in an enclosed container which is heated to vaporize a liquid. The vapor molecules cannot escape the container, so some remain in the space above the liquid and some go back into the liquid. When the volume of those evaporating equals the volume of those condensing, a **dynamic equilibrium** is reached so that the rate of evaporation equals the rate of condensation.

Boiling point is the temperature at which the vapor pressure of the liquid is just equal to the external pressure. The boiling point of a liquid at a pressure of 1 atm is the normal boiling point of that liquid. At higher external pressures, a liquid's boiling point increases. The temperature of a boiling liquid never rises above its boiling point.

The particles in **solids** are tightly packed against each other, so that instead of random movements the particles in solids vibrate and rotate about fixed points. Solids are dense and incompressible and do not flow.

Most solids are crystalline. In **crystals** the atoms, ions, or molecules are arranged in an orderly, repeating, three-dimensional pattern called the crystal lattice. Each substance has a specific characteristic crystal lattice shape that does not vary. There are seven crystal systems that differ based on the angles between the faces and how many of the edges of the faces are equal. The seven crystal shapes are cubic, tetragonal, orthorhombic, monoclinic, triclinic, hexagonal, and rhombohedral.

The unit cell is the smallest group of particles within a crystal that retains the geometric shape of the crystal. Each crystal system has one to four types of unit cells. For example, there are three unit cells that are part of the cubic crystal system: cubic, face-centered cubic, and body-centered cubic. The melting points of crystals are determined by how the atoms are bonded.

When a solid is heated, its particles vibrate faster and the kinetic energy increases. The **melting point** is the temperature at which the solid turns into a liquid because the vibrations of some of the particles are strong enough to overcome the interactions that hold them in fixed positions. The melting point is the same as the freezing point.

Some substances such as carbon can exist in more than one type of solid state. Under tremendous pressure it crystallizes into diamond (compact symmetrical), but under less pressure it crystallizes into graphite (sheets with weak bonds). Soot is also carbon, but with the atoms randomly bonded to one another.

Some solids are **amorphous** and lack an ordered internal structure. Examples are rubber, plastic, and asphalt. Another amorphous solid is glass which does not melt at a specific temperature but gradually soften when heated.

Sublimation is the phase change from solid to vapor without going through liquid. A good example is dry ice, CO_2.

Phase Changes

A phase change occurs when the physical state of a substance changes such as a solid melting to liquid or a gas condensing to liquid.

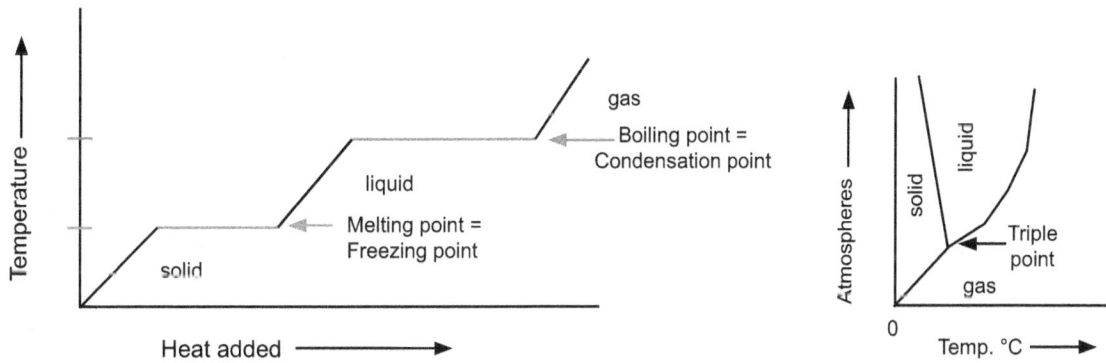

When a phase change occurs the temperature of the substance remains constant. As heat is absorbed the energy causes a change of state instead of a change of temperature. The **heat of fusion** is the heat required to melt one gram of a solid at its melting point. The heat of fusion of water is 80 cal/g, the energy to change 1 g of ice to 1 g water at 0°C. The heat of fusion equals the **heat of solidification**, the amount of heat given up as one gram of liquid changes to a solid at the melting point. The heat of vaporization is the heat required to change 1 g of a liquid to gas at the boiling point of that liquid. For water, the **heat of vaporization** is 540 cal/g. The **heat of condensation** equals the heat of vaporization. It is the heat released when 1 g of a gas condenses to a liquid at the boiling point. The **triple point** is the temperature and pressure at which solid, liquid and gas are in equilibrium.

<u>Example:</u> *Calculate the energy required to change 40 g of ice at -27°C to steam at 150°C.*

Heat 40 g of ice from -27°C to 0°C: (40 g)(1 cal/g°C)(27°C) = 1,080 cal = 1.08 kcal
Phase change 40 g ice to water at 0°C: (40 g)(80 cal/g) = 3,200 cal = 3.20 kcal
Heat 40 g of water from 0°C to 100°C: (40 g)(1 cal/g°C)(100°C) = 4,000 cal = 4.00 kcal
Phase change 40 g water to 40 g steam at 100°C: (40 g)(540 cal/g) = 21,600 cal = 21.60 kcal
Heat 40 g steam to 150°C: (40 g)(1 cal/g°C)(50°C) = 2,000 cal = 2.00 kcal 40 g of ice at -27°C to steam at 150°C: 1.08 kcal + 3.20 kcal + 4.00 kcal + 21.6 kcal + 2.00 kcal = 31.88 kcal of energy

Solutions

Aqueous solutions are water samples containing dissolved substances. The dissolving medium (water) is called the **solvent** and the dissolved particles of a substance are called the **solute**. The **rate of solubility** can be increased by (1) increasing the temperature, (2) agitating by stirring or shaking the solution, or (3) decreasing the solute particle size to create more surface area.

Water molecules are dipoles, so molecules which are dipoles dissolve well in it. With all the molecules in constant motion, it is easy for the H+ end of H2O to attract the negative ions and the O-2 end of H2O to attract the positive ions, thus breaking the bonds between positive and negative ions of the solute. **Solvation** occurs when those ions are surrounded by water molecules. Sometimes ionic compounds have stronger attractive forces than the attractive forces exerted by water. Those compounds, like barium sulfate and calcium carbonate, are insoluble ionic compounds.

Nonpolar molecules do not dissolve much in water, but must be dissolved in a nonpolar solvent such as benzene. As a rule, "like dissolves like" hold true since polar solvents like water dissolve polar and ionic compounds and nonpolar solvents dissolve nonpolar and organic compounds.

Solid, liquid, and gaseous solutions exist. Metal alloys are solid solutions and air is a gaseous solution. Liquids that are soluble in one another are **miscible**. Polar liquids are usually miscible with water, but nonpolar liquids tend to be immiscible with water. The solubilities of gases are greater in cold water than in hot water as the dissolved gases tend to escape the water as vapor. **Henry's Law** applies to gases in liquids: at a given temperature the solubility of a gas in a liquid (S) is directly proportional to the pressure of the gas above the liquid (P) such that $S_1P_2 = S_2P_1$.

The solubility of a substance is the amount of substance that dissolves in a given quantity of a given solvent at a given temperature to produce a saturated solution. A saturated solution contains the maximum amount of solute for a given amount of solvent at a constant temperature and pressure. In a saturated solution the dissolved and undissolved solute are in dynamic equilibrium. Some solutions can be supersaturated under special conditions, allowing more solute than the solvent can theoretically hold to be dissolved. An unsaturated solution is one that contains less than the maximum amount of solute for that amount of that solvent at that temperature and pressure.

Concentrations – Molarity, Molality, and Normality

The **concentration** of a solution is a measure of the amount of solute that is dissolved in a standard quantity of solvent. The terms dilute (small amount of solute) and concentrated (large of amount of solute) are qualitative and not quantitative and therefore, not useful in chemistry.

The most important unit of concentration is **molarity** (*M*) which is the number of moles of a solute dissolved in 1 liter of solution (not solvent, but total solution).

Molarity (*M*) = $\dfrac{\text{number of moles of solute}}{\text{number of liters of solution}}$

Example: *A saline solution ncontains 0.90 g of NaCl per 100 mL of solution. What is its molarity?* Remember the gram formula mass of NaCl is 58.5 g/mol

$M = (0.90 \text{ g})(1 \text{mol}/58.5 \text{ g}) / (100 \text{ mL})(1 \text{ L}/1000 \text{ mL}) = 0.15 \; M \text{ solution}$

The number of moles of solute does not change when a solution is diluted. Changing the quantity of solvent does not change the quantity of solute. Therefore, $M_1V_1 = M_2V_2$.

Another method of expressing concentration is **percent** which can be volume/volume or mass/volume percent. Percent by volume means **volume of solute divided by volume of total solution, then multiplied by 100%**.

Equivalents are used to express concentration for acid-base neutralizations. The mass of one equivalent of a substance is called its gram equivalent mass. One **equivalent** is the amount of an acid (or base) that will give one mole of hydrogen (or hydroxide) ions. One mole of HBr is one equivalent of HBr, so its **gram equivalent mass** is 90 grams. However, one mole of H_2SO_4 is two equivalents (has two hydrogens), so its gram formula mass of 98 grams is double its gram equivalent mass of 49 grams. **Normality** (N) of a solution is the **number of equivalents of solute in 1 L of solution**, or **molarity times the number of ionizable hydrogens**. Dilutions can be made using the formula: $N^1V^1 = N^2V^2$.

A fourth method of expressing concentration is **molality** (*m*) which is **moles of solute per kilogram (1000 g) of solvent**.

 Colligative Properties

The boiling point of a solution is higher than the boiling point of the pure solvent. Adding a solute to the solvent decreases the solvent's vapor pressure, so additional kinetic energy must be added to raise the vapor pressure of the liquid phase to atmospheric pressure. The boiling point of water increases by 0.52°C for every mole of particles that the solute forms when dissolved in 1000 g of water. Since the boiling point of water is dependent on the number of particles dissolved in a given mass of solvent, it is a **colligative property**. The amount of **boiling point elevation** is directly proportional to the molal concentration such that
$\Delta T_b = K_b\, m$

The proportionality constant K_b is in the units °C/molal and is specific to the solvent. Once the ΔT_b has been calculated, it must be <u>added to the normal boiling point</u> of that solvent to get the new boiling point. The K_b for water is 0.512 °C/m.

Adding a solute to a solvent disrupts the pattern of the crystal lattice. More kinetic energy must be withdrawn from the solution than from the pure solvent for solidification to occur. The difference in temperature between the freezing point of the solvent and the freezing point of the solution is the **freezing point depression**. This is a colligative property since it is dependent on the number of particles of solute. This amount is

calculated like the boiling point elevation, but a Kf for the solvent is used and the Δ Tf is subtracted from the normal freezing point of the solvent.
$\Delta T_f = K_f m$ K_f for water is 1.86 °C/m

Raoult's Law uses mole fraction as a measure of concentration when colligative properties like vapor pressure are concerned. Mole fraction is the number of moles of solvent divided by the combined numbers of moles of solvent and solute. Raoult's law says that vapor pressure of the solution is equal to mole fraction of the solvent times the vapor pressure of the solvent.

 Gases

The **Kinetic theory** says that the tiny particles in all forms of matter are in constant motion. These particles may be atoms, ions, or molecules in gases, liquids, or solids. The basic assumptions of the kinetic theory of gases are that (1) a gas is composed of tiny particles (molecules or atoms) of negligible size with distance between them, (2) the particles in a gas move rapidly in constant random motion and collide with each other, and (3) all the collisions are perfectly elastic. The behavior of gases depends on their volume, temperature, and pressure.

The energy an object has because of its motion is called kinetic energy. The average kinetic energy of the particles of a substance is proportional to the temperature of the substance. As the temperature rises, the particles move faster due to increased thermal energy. This causes an increased number of collisions. The collisions produce a measurable force known as pressure.

The volume of a gas is usually measured at **STP, standard temperature (0° Celsius or 273° Kelvin) and pressure (1 atmosphere)**. At STP one mole of any gas occupies a volume of **22.4** liters, a quantity known as the **molar volume** of the given gas.

Example 1: *What is the volume at STP of 3.20×10^{-2} mol CO_2?*
$(3.20 \times 10^{-2}$ mol $CO_2)(22.4$ L CO_2 / 1 mol $CO_2) = 0.717$ L CO_2

Example 2: *Assuming STP, how many moles are in 5.42×10^{-1} mL Ne?*
$(5.42 \times 10^{-1}$ mL Ne$)(1$ L / 1000 mL$)(1$ mol Ne / 22.4 L Ne$) = 2.42 \times 10^{-5}$ mol Ne

The **density of a gas** is usually measured in grams per liter. The experimentally determined density of a gas at STP is used to calculate the gram formula mass of that gas which can be an element or a compound.

<u>Example</u>: *The density of a gas is 2.86 g/L at STP. Determine the gram formula mass of the compound. Is it ammonia (NH_4), sulfur dioxide (SO_2), or methane (CH_4)?*

$$(22.4 \text{ L}/1 \text{ mol})(2.86 \text{ g/L}) = 64.1 \text{ g/mol}$$
$$NH_4 = (1)(14 \text{ g/mol}) + (4)(1 \text{ g/mol}) = 14 \text{ g/mol} + 4 \text{ g/mol} = 18 \text{ g/mol}$$
$$SO_2 = (1)(32 \text{ g/mol}) + (2)(16 \text{ g/mol}) = 32 \text{ g/mol} + 32 \text{ g/mol} = 64 \text{ g/mol}$$
$$CH_4 = (1)(12 \text{ g/mol}) + (4)(1 \text{ g/mol}) = 12 \text{ g/mol} + 4 \text{ g/mol} = 16 \text{ g/mol}$$

Therefore, the compound is SO_2.

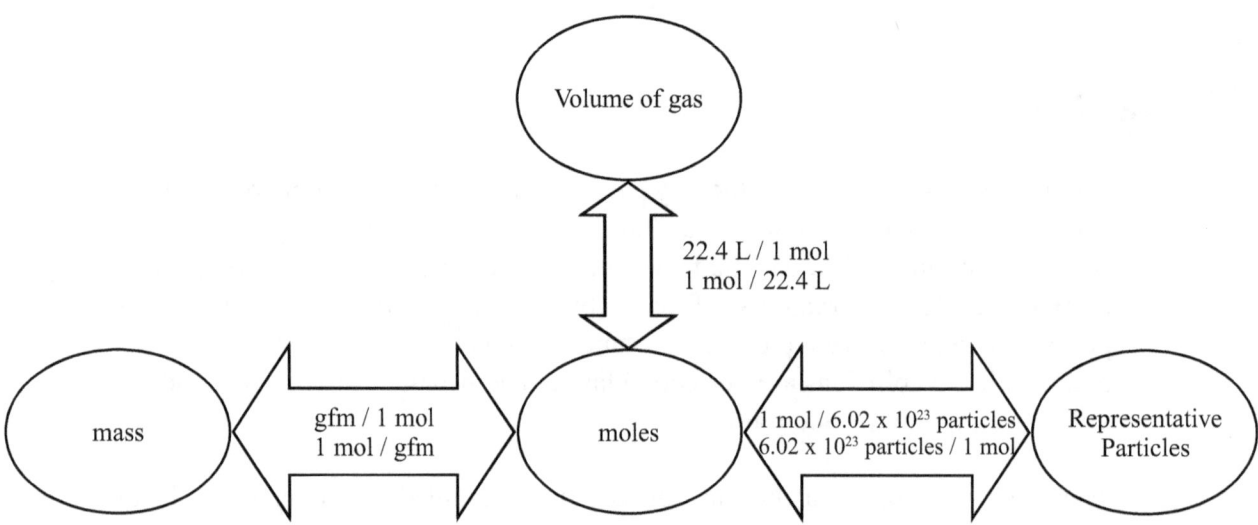

Gas Laws

The gas laws are a set of equations that apply equally to all gases and show relationships among pressure, volume, temperature, moles, and number of particles. A few conversions and constants need to be remembered:

1 atmosphere (atm) = 760 mm Hg Kelvin (K) = °C + 273
Ideal gas constant (R) = 0.082 L-atm/K-mol

Dalton's Law of Partial Pressures: Gases in a single container all have the same volume and are at the same temperature, so the difference in their partial pressures is due only to the difference in the numbers of molecules present. $P_{total} = P_1 + P_2 + P_3 \ldots$

Boyle's Law: At a constant temperature, the pressure of a gas will vary inversely with the volume. In other words, if a given volume of gas has more pressure exerted upon it, it will take less volume. $P_1V_1 = P_2V_2$

Charles' Law: At a constant pressure, the volume of a given amount of gas will vary proportionately with the temperature expressed in Kelvin. Expressed differently, increasing the temperature of a given volume of gas will cause the molecules to move faster and take up more volume. $V_1T_2 = V_2T_1$

Avogadro's Law: Equal volumes of all gases contain the same number of molecules such that **V/n = constant (22.4 liters/mole)**.

Boyle's Law and Charles' Law become the **Combined Gas Law: $P_1V_1T_2 = P_2V_2T_1$**. The **Ideal Gas Equation** combines this and Avogadro's Law as **PV = nRT** where n is the number of particles and R is a constant called the ideal gas constant whose value depends on the units used.

> Example 1: *The pressure in an automobile tire is 2.0 atm at 27°C. At the end of a journey on a hot sunny day the pressure has risen to 2.2 atm. Assuming the volume has not changed, what is the temperature of the air in the tire? Use the combined gas law, but drop out volume:*
>
> $P_1V_1T_2 = P_2V_2T_1$ so it becomes $P_1T_2 = P_2T_1$ or $T_2 = P_2T_1 / P_1$
> $T_2 = (2.2$ atm$)(27°C + 273$ K$) / 2.0$ atm $= 330.0$ K or $(330-273) = 57°C$

> Example 2: *What volume will 12.0 g of oxygen gas occupy at 25°C and a pressure of 0.520 atm?*
>
> PV = nRT (0.520 atm)(V) = (12.0 g O2)(1 mole O2/32 g O2)(0.0821 L-atm/K-mol) (25 + 273 K)
> V = 17.6 L O_2

The particles of ideal gases have no volume and no attraction, but real gases have both volume and mutual attraction. At high pressures and low temperatures, these two factors affect the behavior of gases. At normal laboratory conditions most common gases act like ideal gases. The lower the critical temperature of a gas, the more nearly it behaves as an ideal gas.

Acids and Bases

Historically there are three definitions of acids and bases:

	Arrhenius	Bronsted-Lowry	Lewis
Acid definition	H+	H+ donor	Electron pair acceptor
Base definition	OH-	H+ acceptor	Electron pair donor

In the broadest definition, the Lewis definition, the acid is seen as becoming more negative and the base is seen as becoming more positive.

Arrhenius said all acids must start with H+ and all bases must end with OH-. He believed that an acid like HC_1 had one proton or H+ to donate so it was monoprotic. In the same way, H_2SO_4 had two so it was diprotic and H_3PO_4 had three so it was triprotic.

Acids did not have to have a bases to go with them and bases did not necessarily have acids with them.

The Bronsted-Lowry definition looked at an equation rather than a formula. Acid-base equations had conjugate acid-base pairs:

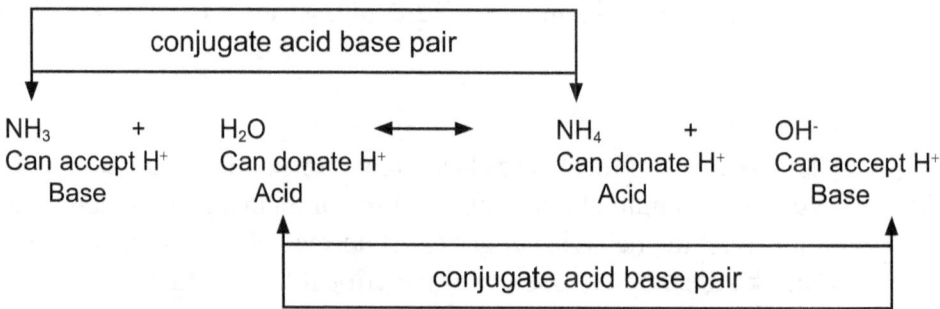

The Lewis dot structures are useful to Lewis' definition. In the equation

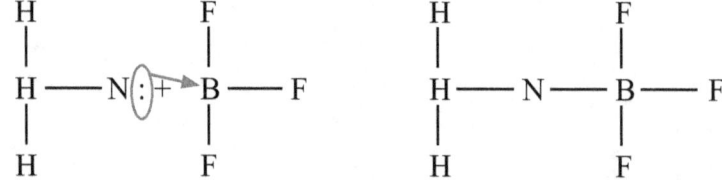

Ammonia is donating a pair of electrons, making it a Lewis base. Boron trifluoride is accepting a pair of electrons, making it a Lewis acid.

Aqueous solutions of acids conduct electricity, so are electrolytes. Aqueous solutions of bases are also electrolytes. Many metals like magnesium react with aqueous solutions of acids to produce hydrogen gas. <u>Acids react with bases to form water and a salt.</u>

Amphoteric means that a substance can be an acid or a base depending on its circumstances. For example, water can donate a H⁺ which makes it an acid or it can accept a H+ which makes it a base. A water molecule that loses a hydrogen ion becomes a negatively charged hydroxide ion (OH^-). A water molecule that gains a hydrogen ion becomes a positively charged hydronium ion (H_3O^+). The reaction in which two wataer molecules react to give ions is the self-ionization of water: $H_2O \leftrightarrow H+ + OH^-$. In pure water (a neutral solution) the concentration of hydrogen ions, [H⁺], and the concentration of hydroxide ions, [OH⁻], are equal at only 1.0 x 10-7 mol/L each. If [H⁺] increases, then [OH⁻] decreases. If additional ions if either type are added to the solution, the equilibrium shifts away from the ion side of the equation.

pH and pOH

The product of the concentrations of the hydrogen ions and the hydroxide ions in water is K_w, the ion-product constant for water: [H⁺] x [OH-] = 1.0 x 10^{-14} mol/L = K_w

The pH scale is the method for expressing the hydrogen ion concentration and the pOH scale is the method for expressing the hydroxide ion concentration.

pH	0	1	2	3	4	5	6	7	8	9	10	11	12	13	14
[H⁺]	10^0	10^{-1}	10^{-2}	10^{-3}	10^{-4}	10^{-5}	10^{-6}	10^{-7}	10^{-8}	10^{-9}	10^{-10}	10^{-11}	10^{-12}	10^{-13}	10^{-14}
Acid								neutral							Base
[OH⁻]	10^{-14}	10^{-13}	10^{-12}	10^{-11}	10^{-10}	10^{-9}	10^{-8}	10^{-7}	10^{-6}	10^{-5}	10^{-4}	10^{-3}	10^{-2}	10^{-1}	10^0
pOH	14	13	12	11	10	9	8	7	6	5	4	3	2	1	0

pH = - log [H⁺]   and   pOH = - log [OH⁻]
pH = - log (1 x 10^{-4})   and   pOH = - log (1 x 10^{-10})
pH = 4   and   pOH = 10   The pH + pOH must = 14

A pH below 7 is acid and corresponds to a pOH above 7. A pOH below 7 is basic and corresponds to a pH above 7.

Precipitates and Salts

Predicting the identity of a precipitate, a solid product in a reaction, requires knowledge of the solubilities of common ionic substances. There are six rules for solubility of salts in water:

1. Most NO_3^- salts are soluble.
2. Most salts of Na^+, K^+, and NH_4^+ are soluble.
3. Most chloride salts are soluble except $AgCl$, $PbCl_2$, and Hg_2Cl_2.
4. Most sulfate salts are soluble except $BaSO_4$, $PbSO_4$, and $CaSO_4$.
5. Most hydroxide salts are only slightly soluble, but important soluble hydroxides are $NaOH$, KOH, and $Ca(OH)_2$.
6. Most sulfide, carbonate, and phosphate salts are only slightly soluble.

Common Ion Effect and Buffers

Buffers are solutions in which the pH remains relatively constant when small amounts of acid or base are added. A buffer is a solution of a weak acid (such as acetic acid, CH3COOH) and one of its salts (such as its anion, CH3COO-). It could also be a solution of a weak base and one of its salts. A buffer solution is better able to resist drastic changes in pH than pure water.

Writing Equations for Chemical Reactions

Chemical reactions involve changes in substances due to the rearrangement of atoms. Bonds are broken and new bonds are formed. Equations use an arrow to the right (→) to indicate a process taking place. No atoms are created or destroyed, thereby obeying the **law of conservation of mass**. Each element has the same number of total atoms on the left of the arrow as it has on the right of the arrow when the equation is balanced.

Some reactants are solids (*s*) which are dissolved in aqueous (*aq*) solution. Some products are precipitates which are solids (*s*). Products which are gases usually are given off into the atmosphere, shown by ↑ or (*g*).

 Predicting Reactions: Reaction Types

Synthesis or Combination: Putting together a compound from the elements (A + B → C) or from a compound and an element (A + BC → D). This is a single product from two reactants.

    <u>Examples</u>: $N_2 + 3\ H_2 \rightarrow 2\ NH_3$ <u>OR</u> $ZnS + 2\ O_2 \rightarrow ZnSO_4$

Decomposition: The opposite of synthesis – this is the coming apart of a compound into two elements or an element and a compound or two compounds. This is a single reactant with two products: C → A + B

    <u>Example 1</u>: $2\ H_2O \rightarrow 2\ H_2 + O_2$ <u>OR</u> $NH_4NO_3 \rightarrow N_2O + 2\ H_2O$

    <u>Example 2</u>: $Na_2CO_3 \rightarrow Na_2O + CO_2\uparrow$ <u>OR</u> $MgSO_4 \rightarrow MgO + SO_3$

Decomposition of –ate polyatomic ions results in a metal oxide and water or carbon dioxide or sulfur trioxide.

Single Replacement: This is an element and a compound with the element replacing one of the elements in the compound so that the products are also a compound and an element. A + BC → AC + B

    <u>Example</u>: $Zn\ (s) + H_2SO_4\ (aq) \rightarrow ZnSO_4\ (aq) + H_2\uparrow$
                  A single replacement reaction involving a metal and water yields a metal hydroxide and hydrogen gas: $Ca + 2\ H_2O \rightarrow Ca(OH)_2 + H_2\uparrow$

Double Displacement or Double Replacement: This is two compounds switching ions or polyatomic ions and becoming two different compounds. AB + CD → AD + CB

    <u>Example</u>: $SrBr_2 + (NH_4)2CO_3 \rightarrow SrCO_3 + 2\ NH_4Br$
                  Note: Double displacement reactions are not oxidation-reduction reactions.

Combustion: This is a burning by use of oxygen of something usually organic (a combination of carbon and hydrogen) which produces carbon dioxide and water.

    <u>Example</u>: $CH_4 + 2\ O_2 \rightarrow CO_2 + 2\ H_2O$

 # Balancing Chemical Equations

1. Determine the correct formulas for all reactants and products, using subscripts to balance ionic charges.
2. Write formulas for reactants on the left of the arrow and predict the products and write their formulas to the right of the arrow.
3. Under the reactants list all the elements in the reactants, starting with metals, then nonmetals, listing oxygen last and hydrogen next to last. Under the products, list all the elements in the same order as those under the reactants (straight across from them).
4. Count the atoms of each element on the left side and list the numbers next to the elements. Repeat for products. Don't forget that subscripts outside a parenthesis multiply everything inside the parenthesis including subscripts inside the parenthesis.
5. For the first element in the list that has unequal numbers of atoms, use a coefficient (numeral to the left of the compound or element) to give the correct number of atoms. NEVER change the subscripts to balance an equation.
6. Go to the next unbalanced element and balance it, moving down the list until all are balanced.
7. Start back at the beginning of the list and actually count the atoms of each element on each side of the arrow to make sure the number listed is the actual number. Rebalance and re-check as needed.

Example: $Al(OH)_3 + NaOH \rightarrow NaAlO_2 + 2\ H_2O$

Al = 1   Al = 1
Na = 1   Na = 1
H = 3 + 1 = 4 H = ~~2~~ 4
O = 3 + 1 = 4 O = ~~2 + 1 = 3~~ 2 + 2 = 4
                Put a 2 in front of H_2O

 # Stoichiometry

Stoichiometry is the calculation of theoretical quantities associated with chemical equations. Coefficients and subscripts tell how many atoms there are of each element. Coefficients tell how many moles there are of each element. Chemical equations must obey the **law of conservation of mass** and the **law of conservation of atoms** for each element in the equation in that masses and numbers of atoms of each element must be equal on the two sides of the arrow. (Mass and numbers of atoms cannot be created or lost.)

Stoichiometry can be used to calculate the amount in mass or moles of a product formed from a given mass or moles of a reactant or the amount (mass or moles) of a reactant needed to obtain a specific amount (mass or moles) of a product. As well as massmass and mass-mole problems, it can be used for mass-volume, volume-volume, and particle-mass calculations.

The general format is to write the correctly balanced equation with correct formulas. List the "given" information. Then list what is needed. Either start with moles of the given or use the gram formula mass of the given to convert it to moles. Convert moles of given to moles of unknown. Then, if mass of unknown is needed, use the gram formula mass to obtain it from the moles.

Example: *How many grams of nitrogen are needed to produce 34.0 g of NH_3?*

$$\text{? g} \qquad 34.0 \text{ g}$$
Write Equation: $N_2 + 3 H_2 \rightarrow 2 NH_3$

Above equation, put givens and unknowns

List what is given and what is unknown:
Mass NH_3: 34.0 g
GFM NH_3: 17.0 g/mol
Moles NH_3: 2 (coefficient)

Mass N_2: unknown
GFM N_2: 28.0 g/mol
Moles N_2: 1 (no coefficient)

Use the label canceling method:

$$34.0 \text{ g } \cancel{NH_3} \times \frac{1 \text{ mole } \cancel{NH_3}}{17.0 \text{ g } \cancel{NH_3}} \times \frac{1 \text{ mole } N_2}{2 \text{ moles } \cancel{NH_3}} \times \frac{28.0 \text{ g } N_2}{1 \text{ mol } \cancel{N_2}} \quad ---$$

Notice "given" x gfm given x mole ration x gfm unknown = "unknown"

Because the gfm means that a certain number of grams equals one mole, either the grams can be put on top with the mol on the bottom of the fraction or the mol can be put on top with the grams on the bottom.

In this example, use a calculator to multiply 34.0 times 28.0 (times any other numbers on the top that are not 1) to get 952.0, leave it on the calculator screen, then divide by 17.0 and divide by 2 (if there are any numbers other than 1, divide by those numbers) to get the answer of 28.0 g N_2.

If a gas is involved, use 22.4 liters/mol instead of gram formula mass. If the previous example wants the unknown as liters, the last step would be 22.4 L/mol instead of 28.0 g/mol and the answer would be 22.4 liters. If both the given and unknown are expressed in liters, only the mole ratio must be performed since the 22.4 L/1 mol would cancel the 1 mol/22.4 L in the problem. For 34.0 L of NH_3 to be formed, 17.0 L of N_2 would be needed. To get the number of molecules or formula units, use 6.02×10^{23} particles per mol into the equation.

Limiting Reagent

In a reaction, any reactant that is used up completely is the **limiting reagent**. All reactants that are not used up completely are referred to as being in excess.

Example: What is the maximum number of grams of Cu_2S that can be formed when 80.0 g of Cu reacts with 25.0 g of S?

Write Equation:
$$\underset{2\ Cu\ +}{80.0\ g} \quad \underset{S\ \rightarrow}{25.0\ g} \quad \underset{Cu_2S}{?\ g}$$

Above equation, put givens and unknowns

The problem must be worked twice, once from copper to copper(I) sulfide and once from sulfur to copper(I) sulfide. The amount of copper(I) sulfide produced, the actual answer to the problem, will be the smaller of the numbers obtained.

List what is given and what is unknown:

Mass Cu: 80.0 g
GFM Cu: 63.55 g/mol
Moles Cu: 2 (coefficient)

Mass Cu_2S: unknown
GFM Cu_2S: 159.16 g/mol
Moles Cu_2S: 1 (no coefficient)

Use the label canceling method:

$$80.0\ g\ Cu \times \frac{1\ mole\ Cu}{63.55\ g\ Cu} \times \frac{1\ mole\ Cu_2S}{2\ moles\ Cu} \times \frac{159.16\ g\ Cu_2S}{1\ mol\ Cu_2S}$$

Use a calculator to multiply 80.0 times 159.16 to get 12732.8, leave it on the calculator screen, then divide by 63.55 and divide by 2 to get the answer of 100.18 g Cu_2S

List what is given and what is unknown:

Mass S: 25.0 g
GFM S: 32.06 g/mol
Moles S: 1 (no coefficient)

Mass Cu_2S: unknown
FM Cu_2S: 159.16 g/mol
Moles Cu_2S: 1 (no coefficient)

Use the label canceling method:

$$25.0 \text{ g S} \times \frac{1 \text{ mole S}}{32.06 \text{ g S}} \times \frac{1 \text{ mole } Cu_2S}{1 \text{ moles S}} \times \frac{159.16 \text{ g } Cu_2S}{1 \text{ mol } Cu_2S}$$

Use a calculator to multiply 25.0 times 159.16 to get 3979.0, leave it on the calculator screen, then divide by 32.06 to get the answer of 124.11 g Cu_2S.

The 80.0 g of Cu will yield 100.18 g Cu_2S if there is excess S while the 25.0 g S will yield 124.11 g Cu_2S if there is excess Cu. Therefore, since the Cu yields the lesser amount of Cu_2S, it is the limiting reagent and the 100.18 g Cu2S will be the yield of the reaction.

Theoretical Yield, Actual Yield, and Percent Yield

Using stoichiometry gives the **theoretical yield** of a reaction – that is, the most that the reaction would yield if all conditions were absolutely perfect. However, in reality there is never a time when all the conditions are absolutely perfect, so what is obtained is called the **actual yield**. The ratio of the actual yield to the theoretical yield is called the **percent yield**. It measures the efficiency of the reaction. A percent yield would normally be less than 100%. Reasons for that are that the reaction may reach equilibrium, the reactants may not be pure, there may be error in measurement, or there may be competing side reactions.

$$\text{Percent yield} = \frac{\text{actual yield}}{\text{theoretical yield}} \times 100\%$$

In the reaction in the preceding example, the theoretical yield is 100.18 g Cu_2S. If the reaction was performed in a lab, the lab tech got 89.5 g Cu_2S. Therefore, the percent yield is (89.5/100.18)(100%) = 89.3%.

 Oxidation-Reduction Equations and Net Ionic Equations

Oxidation numbers are a method for tracking electrons in a chemical equation. Some ions always have the same oxidation number, but many can change oxidation numbers depending on what other ions are in the compound. The sum of the oxidation numbers (times the subscripts for those ions) of a compound must equal zero. (1) To determine oxidation numbers, start by placing the oxidation number above those ions whose oxidation number does not change – any ion from Group 1A is +1, from 2A is +2, from 6A is -2, and from 7A is -1. (2) Any uncombined element (listed by itself) is 0. (3)

Hydrogen is always +1 except in a metal hydride (NaH) when it is -1. (4) Oxygen is always -2 except in hydrogen peroxide, H_2O_2, when it is -1. (5) In polyatomic ions, the sum of the oxidation numbers must equal the charge on the polyatomic ion.

> Example 1: In SO_2, each oxygen is -2, so the net negative charge is -4, giving a net positive charge of +4. Each sulfur is +4.

> Example 2: In NH_4, each hydrogen is -1 for a total of -4, but the charge on the polyatomic ion is +1, so N must be +5.

> Example 3: For $Na_2Cr_2O_7$ the oxygens are -2 each for a total of (7)(-2) = -14 and the sodiums are each +1 for a total of (2)(+1) = +2. That is a difference of -12. There are 2 chromiums, so (-12)/(2) = -6 for each chromium.

The total number of electrons on the left of the equation must equal the total number of electrons on the right. A *decrease* in an element's oxidation number from the left of the arrow (reactants) to the right of the arrow (products) signifies **reduction**. An *increase* in an element's oxidation number left to right signifies **oxidation**. The element undergoing the reduction is reduced and serves as the oxidizing agent (electron acceptor). The element undergoing the oxidation is oxidized and serves as the reducing agent (electron donor). Reduction and oxidation (known as redox) go hand-in-hand in an equation, one cannot happen without the other also happening.

> Example 1: In the equation $Cl_2 + 2\ HBr \rightarrow 2\ HCl + Br_2$, both Cl_2 and Br_2 will be zero and H will be +1, making Br^1 and Cl^{-1}. That means that chlorine goes from 0 to -1, so it is reduced, and bromine goes from -1 to 0 so it is oxidized.

Example 2: Zinc is oxidized (0 → +2) and manganese is reduced (+4 → +3) in: Zn + 2 MnO_2 + 2 NH_4Cl → $ZnCl_2$ + Mn_2O_3 + 2 NH_3 + H_2O

Balancing redox equations can be tricky, but if the electrons are balanced, the coefficients are easier to balance. Once oxidation numbers have been assigned to all the elements on both sides of the equation and the atoms oxidized and reduced have been identified, use coefficients to make the total increase in oxidation number (loss of electrons) equal to the total decrease in oxidation number (gain of electrons). Then balance the equation as normal.

Example: Ca + 2 H_2O → $Ca(OH)_2$ + H_2
           0   +1 -2   +2 -2 +1 0

Ca: 0 → +2, so add electrons (e-) to right side to make it equal 0
H: +1 → 0, so add electrons to left side to make it equal 0
Ca: 0 → +2 + 2 e-
H: +1 + 1 e- → 0   multiply this half-reaction by 2 so the numbers of electrons are equal, then put that 2 in front of the H_2O

Net ionic reaction: Ca^0 + 2 H_2+1 + 1 e- → Ca^{+2} + H_2 + 1 e-

Spectator ions are those ions that are unchanged. In this case, O-2.

Now see how close to balanced the equation is:

     Ca = 1   Ca = 1
     H = 4   H = 2 + 2 = 4
     O = 2   O = 2

Reaction Rate, Equilibrium, and Catalysts

A dynamic equilibrium consists of two **opposing reversible processes** that both occur at the same rate. When a process at equilibrium is observed, it often doesn't seem like anything is happening, but at a microscopic scale, two events are taking place that balance each other - the forward reaction is occurring at a rate equal to the rate of the reverse reaction. In order for one species to be converted to another during a chemical reaction, the reactants must collide. The collisions between the reactants determine how fast the reaction takes place. However, during a chemical reaction, only a fraction of the collisions between the appropriate reactant molecules convert them into product molecules. This occurs for two reasons:

1) Not all collisions occur with a **sufficiently high energy** for the reaction to occur.
2) Not all collisions **orient the molecules properly** for the reaction to occur.

The **activation energy**, E_a, of a reaction is the **minimum energy to overcome the barrier to the formation of products** and allow the reaction to occur. The activation energy, E_a, is the difference between the energy of reactants and the energy of the activated complex. The energy change during the reaction, ΔE, is the difference between the energy of the products and the energy of the reactants. The activation energy of the reverse reaction is $E_a - \Delta E$. These energy levels are represented in the energy diagrams shown below:

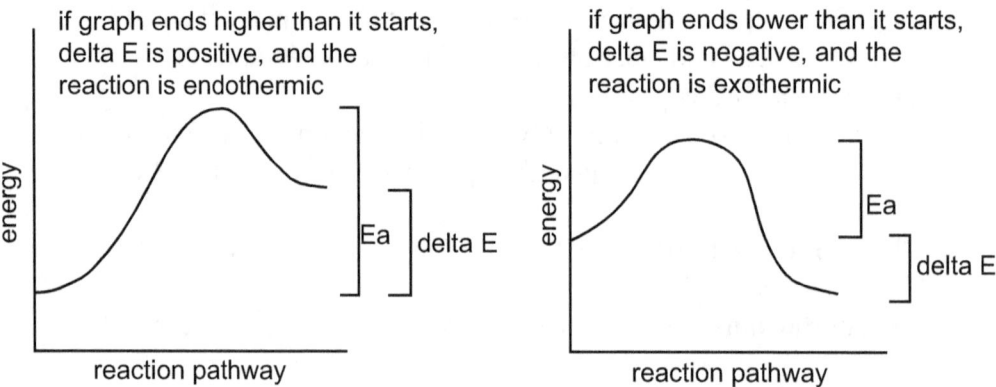

A **catalyst** is an element or compound that is added to the reaction to (1) speed the rate of the reaction, (2) make a reaction occur that would not otherwise occur, (3) reduce the minimum activation energy necessary for the reaction to occur, or (4) make a reaction more efficient. When the reaction is finished, the catalyst can be separated out unchanged. A catalyst increases the rate of both the forward and reverse reactions by lowering the activation energy for the reaction.

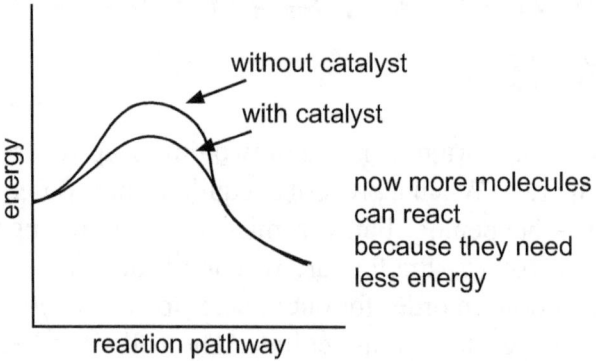

 # Sample Test Questions

1) Every magnet

   A) Has two poles – east and west
   B) Has a field of force which runs from the north to the south pole
   C) Is made of iron
   D) Is a permanent magnet

The correct answer is C:) Is made of iron. Has a field of force with runs from the north to the south pole. Every magnet has two poles, a north pole and a south pole, with a field of force which runs from the north to the south pole.

2) An example of a second class lever is

   A) Pulling a nail using a claw on a hammer head
   B) Raking leaves
   C) Hitting a ball with a bat
   D) Moving mulch with a wheelbarrow

The correct answer is D:) Moving mulch with a wheelbarrow. Moving mulch with a wheelbarrow. In a second class lever the resistance is between the effort and the fulcrum. A wheelbarrow is a good example as the person exerts the effort, the fulcrum is the wheel, and the resistance is the load of mulch between the person and the wheel.

3) A doorknob is an example of a(n)

   A) Pulley
   B) Inclined plane
   C) Wheel and axle
   D) Screw

The correct answer is C:) Wheel and axle. A good everyday example of a wheel and axle is a doorknob.

4) How much work is done when a force of 25 newtons is used to slide a 150-newton sofa 10 meters across the floor?

    A) 250 joules
    B) 15 joules
    C) 1,500 joules
    D) 2.5 joules

The correct answer is A:) 250 joules. Work = force x distance = 25 newtons x 10 meters = 250 joules.

5) Why does a piece of metal feel colder than a piece of wood in the same room?

    A) The metal is colder than the wood.
    B) The wood holds heat better than the metal.
    C) The metal conducts heat away from the body of the person touching it better than the wood does.
    D) The wood serves as a better insulator than the metal.

The correct answer is C:) The metal conducts heat away from the body of the person touching it better than the wood does. Metal feels colder than wood at the same temperature because the metal conducts heat away from the body of the person touching it better than the wood does.

6) Which of the following is NOT a type of heating system?

    A) Hot water
    B) Steam
    C) Solar
    D) Gasoline

The correct answer is D:) Gasoline. Heating systems use hot water, steam, sun or solar energy, air heated with a heat pump or a furnace using natural gas or oil or electricity.

7) Using Ohm's Law, calculate the current through a resistance of 100 ohms when a 12-volt battery is used.

   A) 0.12 amps
   B) 1200 amps
   C) 8.33 amps
   D) 12 amps

The correct answer is A:) 0.12 amps. Current (in amperes) = voltage (in volts) /resistance (in ohms) = 12/100 = 0.12 amps.

8) When an object loses electrons,

   A) It becomes negatively charged
   B) It becomes positively charged
   C) It becomes neutral
   D) It repels all charges

The correct answer is B:) It becomes positively charged. When an object loses negatively charged electrons, the object becomes positively charged.

9) As sound wave frequency increases,

   A) The corresponding wavelength increases
   B) The wavelength is not affected
   C) The wavelength decreases
   D) The sounds cannot be heard through a telephone

The correct answer is C:) The wavelength decreases. As the frequency of a sound wave increases, the wavelength decreases.

10) A person with normal hearing can hear sounds with a frequency range of

   A) 340 to 2,000 hertz
   B) 20 to 1,000 hertz
   C) 1,000 to 20,000 hertz
   D) 20 to 20,000 hertz

The correct answer is D:) 20 to 20,000 hertz. Most people hear compressional or sound waves if their frequency is between about 20 hertz and about 20,000 hertz.

11) A concave lens is used in

   A) A simple telescope
   B) Glasses for a nearsighted person
   C) A camera
   D) A microscope

The correct answer is B:) Glasses for a nearsighted person. Nearsighted vision can be corrected with glasses with concave lenses which produce a clear, sharp imager inside the eye to help with seeing things at a distance.

12) Characteristics of waves do NOT include:

   A) The wavelength is the linear distance of one wave crest and trough
   B) The frequency is the number of waves passing a given point in one second
   C) Refraction occurs when a wave strikes an object and bounces off
   D) The speed of a wave is its wavelength times its frequency

The correct answer is C:) Refraction occurs when a wave strikes an object and bounces off.

13) The Doppler Effect is associated most closely with which property of waves?

   A) Amplitude
   B) Wavelength
   C) Frequency
   D) Intensity

The correct answer is C:) Frequency. The Doppler Effect accounts for an apparent increase in frequency when a wave source moves toward a wave receiver or apparent decrease in frequency when a wave source moves away from a wave receiver.

14) The transfer of heat by electromagnetic waves is called

   A) Conduction
   B) Convection
   C) Phase change
   D) Radiation

The correct answer is D:) Radiation. Heat transfer via electromagnetic waves (which can occur even in a vacuum) is called radiation. Heat transferred by direct contact is conduction, by fluid current is convection, and by matter changing phase is vaporization or melting.

Principles of Physical Science I

15) When heat is added to most solids, they expand because

   A) The molecules get bigger
   B) The molecules form a more rigid structure
   C) The faster molecular motion leads to greater distance between the molecules
   D) The molecules develop greater repelling electric forces

The correct answer is C:) The faster molecular motion leads to greater distance between the molecules. The faster molecular motion leads to a greater distance between the molecules. Temperature is a measure of average kinetic energy of the particles. Warmer molecules have more energy, so move further away from each other. When they bounce into each other, they bounce off with more energy and go further.

16) The force of gravity on earth causes all bodies in free fall to

   A) Fall at the same speed
   B) Fall at a rate proportional to their mass
   C) Accelerate at the same rate
   D) Reach the same terminal velocity

The correct answer is C:) Accelerate at the same rate. Gravity causes approximately the same acceleration on all falling bodies close to earth's surface.

17) Resistance is measured in units called

   A) Watts
   B) Volts
   C) Ohms
   D) Current

The correct answer is C:) Ohms. A watt is a unit of energy. Potential difference is measured in a unit called the volt. Current is the number of electrons per second that flow past a point in a circuit. An ohm is the unit for resistance.

18) Sound can be transmitted in all of the following except

   A) Air
   B) Water
   C) A diamond
   D) A vacuum

The correct answer is D:) A vacuum. Sound, a longitudinal wave, is transmitted by vibrations of molecules, so it can be transmitted through any gas, liquid, or solid. But it cannot be transmitted through a vacuum, because there are no particles present to vibrate and bump into their adjacent particles to transmit the waves.

19) The speed of light is different in different materials. This is responsible for

   A) Interference
   B) Refraction
   C) Reflection
   D) Diffraction

The correct answer is B:) Refraction. Refraction is the bending of light because it hits a material at an angle, giving it a different speed.

20) A converging lens produces a real image

   A) Every time
   B) Never
   C) When the object is within one focal length of the lens
   D) When the object is further than one focal length from the lens

The correct answer is D:) When the object is further than one focal length from the lens. A converging lens produces a real image whenever the object is far enough from the lens (outside one focal length) so that the rays of light from the object can hit the lens and be focused into a real image on the other side of the lens.

21) The electromagnetic radiation with the longest wave length is/are

   A) Radio waves
   B) Infrared light
   C) X-rays
   D) Ultraviolet light

The correct answer is A:) Radio waves. Radio waves have the longest wave lengths. If you do not remember the sequence, you might recall that wave length is inversely proportional to frequency, and that radio waves are considered much less harmful (less energetic, i.e. lower frequency) than ultraviolet or X-ray.

22) Energy is measured with the same units as

   A) Force
   B) Momentum
   C) Work
   D) Power

The correct answer is C:) Work. Energy = (mass) x (length)^2 / time^2 = g –m^2 /s^2 Work = force x distance = N-m = g-m/s x m = g – m^2 / s^2.

23) All of the following are considered Newton's Laws except for:

   A) An object in motion or at rest will continue in motion or at rest unless acted upon by an outside force.
   B) For every action force, there is an equal and opposite reaction force.
   C) Friction is required to keep a car on a curve on the road.
   D) Mass can be considered the ratio of force to acceleration.

The correct answer is C:) Friction is required to keep a car on a curve on the road. However, cars weren't around during Newton's lifetime. Newton's Laws include (1) an object in motion (or at rest) will stay in motion (or at rest) until acted upon by an outside force, (2) force equals mass times acceleration, and (3) for every action there is an equal and opposite reaction.

24) A ball rolls down a smooth hill. You may ignore air resistance. Which of the following is a true statement?

   A) The ball has more energy at the start of its descent than just before it hits the bottom of the hill, because it is higher up at the beginning.
   B) The ball has less energy at the start of its descent than just before it hits the bottom of the hill, because it is moving more quickly at the end.
   C) The ball has the same energy throughout its descent, because potential energy is converted to kinetic energy.
   D) The ball has the same energy throughout its descent, because a single object (such as a ball) cannot gain or lose energy.

The correct answer is C:) The ball has the same energy throughout its descent, because potential energy is converted to kinetic energy. It has more potential energy at the top and more kinetic energy as it rolls down, but the total is the same throughout.

25) To add 3.25×10^5 and 4.5×10^4 you would

   A) Add the numbers and then add the exponents to get 7.75×10^9
   B) Change the exponents to be the same, add the numbers, and then add the exponents to get $32.5 \times 10^4 + 4.5 \times 10^4 = 37 \times 10^8$
   C) Change the exponents to be the same, add the numbers, and use the same exponent so that $32.5 \times 10^4 + 4.5 \times 10^4 = 37.0 \times 10^4$
   D) Change the exponents to be the same, add the numbers, use the same exponent, then put the answer in scientific notation (if it isn't) and round to significant figures such that 3.25×10^5 and $.45 \times 10^5 = 3.70 \times 10^5 = 3.7 \times 10^5$

The correct answer is D:) Change the exponents to be the same, add the numbers, use the same exponent, then put the answer in scientific notation (if it isn't) and round to significant figures such that 3.25×10^5 and $.45 \times 10^5 = 3.70 \times 10^5 = 3.7 \times 10^5$. Even though the answer is essentially the same for C and D, D is more correct because it puts the answer back into scientific notation and significant figures.

26) A runner completes 10 kilometers of a 20-K race in 40 minutes and the second half in 45 minutes. What is his average speed?

   A) 0.25 km/min
   B) 0.22 km/min
   C) 0.24 km/min
   D) 0.12 km/min

The correct answer is C:) 0.24 km/min. S = 20 km/85 min = 0.235 km/min or 0.24 km/min.

27) A 2-kg weight is dropped from rest and lands 5 seconds later. What is its initial velocity?

   A) 9.8 m/s^2
   B) 0.0 m/s^2
   C) 29.4 m/s^2
   D) 49.0 m/s^2

The correct answer is B:) 0.0 m/s^2. Its initial velocity is at rest which is 0.0 m/s.

28) What is the average velocity of the weight in question 27?

   A) 9.8 m/s^2
   B) 49.0 m/s^2
   C) 24.5 m/s^2
   D) 0.0 m/s^2

The correct answer is C:) 24.5 m/s^2. Its final velocity is v_f = 5 sec x 9.8 m/s^2 = 49.0 m/s^2. Its average velocity is v_{av} = $(v_f + v_0) / 2$ = (49.0 m/s^2 + 0)/2 = 24.5 m/s^2.

29) If a ball is dropped from a height of 36 meters, how long will it take to hit the ground?

   A) 7.3 s
   B) 2.7 s
   C) 9.8 s
   D) 3.7 s

The correct answer is B:) 2.7 s. $d = v_0 t + \frac{1}{2} a t^2$. Therefore, 36 m = 0 + ½ (9.8 m/s^2)(t^2). Dividing, you get t^2 = 7.3 s^2. And, take the square root t = 2.7 seconds.

30) What will be the velocity of the ball in question 29 just before it strikes the ground?

   A) 19.6 m/s
   B) 705.6 m/s
   C) 32.6 m/s
   D) 26.6 m/s

The correct answer is D:) 26.6 m/s. Use $v^2 = v_0^2 + 2ad$ to get v^2 = 0 + (2)(9.8 m/s^2)(36 m). Then v^2 = 705.6 m^2/s^2 and v = 26.6 m/s.

31) If a boat is to start on one side of a river flowing 2.7 km/hr and end up directly across river from where it started, it will have to be pointed upstream at some angle. The boat will travel 7.5 km/hr. What will its velocity (which includes direction) need to be relative to the earth?

   A) 8.0 km/hr at an angle of 19.8° upstream
   B) 8.0 km/hr at an angle of 19.8° downstream
   C) 7.5 km/hr at an angle of 21.1° upstream
   D) 7.8 km/hr at an angle of 16.8° upstream

The correct answer is A:) 8.0 km/hr at an angle of 19.8° upstream. Tan Θ = opp/adj = 2.7/7.5 = .36   Θ = 19.8° upstream
Sin Θ = opp/hyp   sin 19.8° = 2.7 km/hr / hyp
0.339 = 2.7/hyp   Hyp = 2.7/.339 = 8.0 km/hr

32) Which has the most momentum?

   A) A 4,000-kg truck moving at 10 km/hr
   B) A 1,800-kg car moving at 14 km/hr
   C) A 3,600-kg truck moving at 8 km/hr
   D) A 1,200-kg car moving at 25 km/hr

The correct answer is A:) A 4,000-kg truck moving at 10 km/hr.
The 4,000-kg truck's momentum = 4,000 kg x 10 km/hr = 40,000 kg-km/hr. The 1,800-kg car's momentum = 1,800 kg x 14 km/hr = 25,200 kg-km/hr. The 3,600-kg truck's momentum = 3,600 kg x 8 km/hr = 28,800 kg-km/hr. The 1,200-kg car's momentum = 1,200 kg x 25 km/hr = 30,000 kg-km/hr.

33) When banking a curve in a road, the angle at which the road should be banked depends on

   A) The mass of the vehicle
   B) The radius of the curve
   C) The speed of the vehicle
   D) The condition of the tires on the vehicle

The correct answer is C:) The speed of the vehicle. The angle at which the road should be banked depends on the speed of the vehicle, but not its mass.

34) A force of 12 N is used to move a box across a horizontal floor a distance of 3 m. If the force makes an angle of 30° with the floor, how much work is done?

A) 36.0 J
B) 101.8 J
C) 31.2 J
D) 4.0 J

The correct answer is C:) 31.2 J. Use W = Fd cos Θ to get W = 12 N x 3 m x 0.866.

35) Power is

A) Work done over a period of time
B) Inversely related to force
C) Measured in newtons
D) Not able to be measured, only calculated

The correct answer is A:) Work done over a period of time. Power is the work done divided by the amount of time that it took to do it. It is measured in joules per second or watts.

36) A pendulum bob is pulled to one side until its center of gravity has been raised 15 cm above its equilibrium position. Find the speed of the bob as it swings through the equilibrium position.

A) 0.17 m/s
B) 1.7 m/s
C) 2.94 m/s
D) 0.75 m/s

The correct answer is B:) 1.7 m/s. PE at top = KE at bottom so mhg = ½ mv² or 2hg = v². Substitute and get (2)(0.15 m)(9.8 m/s²) = v² which becomes 2.94 m²/s² = v². Take the square root: 1.7 m/s = v.

37) Efficiency can be increased by all except

A) Sanding rough edges
B) Greasing bearings
C) Lowering the temperature
D) Decreasing friction

The correct answer is C:) Lowering the temperature. Efficiency is increased by anything that decreases friction such as sanding rough edges or greasing bearings.

38) Temperature is a measure of

   A) Hot and cold
   B) Thermal equilibrium
   C) Kinetic energy of the particles
   D) Potential energy of the particles

The correct answer is C:) Kinetic energy of the particles. Temperature measures the average kinetic energy of the particles in a material.

39) A blacksmith heated an iron bar to 1450° C. The blacksmith then tempered the metal by dropping it into 43,000 cm3 of water that had a temperature of 22° C. The final temperature of the system was 45° C. What was the mass of the bar? (Cp of iron = 0.4494 J/g°C and Cp of water is 4.18 J/g°C)

   A) 1566.0 g
   B) 5682.5 g
   C) 2969.5 g
   D) 1511.3 g

The correct answer is B:) 5682.5 g. q = (m)(ΔT)(Cp) and q iron = q water (heat lost by iron = heat gained by water). The mass of the system is (43,000 g + m) and 1 cm3 = 1 g. (43,000 g + m)(45-22°C)(4.18 J/g°C)= m(1450-45°C)(0.4494 J/g°C) 4,134,020 g + 96.14(m) = -631.40(m) OR 4,134,020 g = -727.5(m).

40) The Laws of Thermodynamics define the relationships among all except

   A) Forms of temperature
   B) Forms of energy
   C) Forms of work
   D) Forms of heat

The correct answer is A:) Forms of temperature. The Laws of Thermodynamics help define the relationships among forms of heat, forms of energy, and forms of work. The First Law says that the change in heat energy supplied to a system is equal to the sum of the change in the internal energy and the change in the work done by the system against internal forces.

41) The energy required to change 50 g of ice at – 25 C to steam at 100 C is

    A) 37.25 kcal
    B) 500 kcal
    C) 27.00 kcal
    D) 12.95 kcal

The correct answer is A:) 37.25 kcal. Heat 50 g ice from -25°C to 0°C:
(50 g)(1 cal/g°C)(25°C) = 1,250 cal = 1.25 kcal Phase change 50 g ice to water at 0°C:
(50 g)(80 cal/g) = 4,000 cal = 4.00 kcal Heat 50 g water from 0°C to 100°C:
(50 g)(1 cal/g°C)(100°C) = 5,000 cal = 5.00 kcal Phase change 50 g water to 50 g steam 100°C:
(50 g)(540 cal/g) = 27.00 kcal
Grand Total: 50 g ice at -25°C to steam at 100°C:
1.25 kcal + 4.00 kcal + 5.00 kcal + 27.00 kcal = 37.25 kcal.

42) The interaction of two or more waves that meet

    A) Is constructive interference if the crest of one meets the trough of another
    B) Produces a wave with lower amplitude that produces a louder sound
    C) Produces a wave of greater amplitude in constructive interference
    D) Produces a louder sound in destructive interference

The correct answer is C:) Produces a wave of greater amplitude in constructive interference. Constructive interference happens when two waves interact so that the crests meet and combine to produce a crest with greater amplitude, making a louder sound. Destructive interference is two waves combined so that the crest of one meets the trough of the other, producing a wave with lower amplitude that gives a softer sound.

43) Conductors

    A) Are nonmetals
    B) Are positively charged materials
    C) Do not allow movement of electrical charges
    D) Allow the movement of electrons through them

The correct answer is D:) Allow the movement of electrons through them. Materials through which electric charges can easily flow are called conductors. Metals (on the left side of the periodic table) are good conductors.

44) The French physicist Coulomb found that the force between two charges Q1 and Q2 is directly proportional to

   A) The product of the charges and inversely proportional to the square of the distance between the charges
   B) The sum of the charges and inversely proportional to the square of the distance between the charges
   C) The square of the charges and inversely proportional to the product of the charges
   D) The square of the distance between the charges and inversely proportional to the product of the charges

The correct answer is A:) The product of the charges and inversely proportional to the square of the distance between the charges. Coulomb found that the force between two charges is directly proportional to the product of the charges and inversely proportional to the square of the distance r between the charges.

45) A 100-watt incandescent lamp operates at 120 volts. What current is drawn?

   A) 1.20 amps
   B) 1.00 amps
   C) 1.50 amps
   D) 0.83 amps

The correct answer is D:) 0.83 amps. Use P = V I to get 100 watts = 120 volts (I). Therefore, 100 watts/120 volts = I and 0.83 amps = I.

46) What is the resistance of the lamp in question 45?

   A) 144.6 ohms
   B) 333.3 ohms
   C) 0.0083 ohms
   D) 99.6 ohms

The correct answer is A:) 144.6 ohms. Use I = V / R to get 0.83 amps = 120 volts / R. Therefore, 120 volts / 0.83 amps = R and 144.6 ohms = R.

47) The type of electric current in a house is

   A) Potential
   B) Direct
   C) Alternating
   D) Series

The correct answer is C:) Alternating. The current in a house is alternating current where the electrons rapidly reverse direction repeatedly.

48) An electromagnet can be made more powerful in all the following ways except

   A) Make more coils.
   B) Put an iron core inside the coils.
   C) Use more air through the coils.
   D) Use more power through the coils.

The correct answer is C:) Use more air through the coils. An electromagnet can be made more powerful by making more coils, putting an iron core inside the coils, or using more power through the coils.

49) A helium nucleus emitted from the nucleus of a radioactive nuclide is called a(n)

   A) Alpha particle
   B) Beta particle
   C) Positron
   D) Gamma ray

The correct answer is A:) Alpha particle. An alpha particle is ^4_2He.

50) What much of a 1600 gram sample of $^{68}_{32}Ge$, whose half-life is about nine months, will remain after 4.5 years?

   A) 4 ½ grams
   B) 25 grams
   C) 50 grams
   D) 30 grams

The correct answer is B:) 25 grams. Four and a half years times twelve months is fifty-four months. 54 months divided by 9 months is 6 half lives. Therefore, at the end of the first half-life (9 months), there is 800 grams. After the second (18 months), 400 grams. After the third (27 months), 200 grams. After the fourth (36 months), 100 grams, and after the fifth (45 months) 50 grams. And after the sixth half-life (54 months) there is 25 grams left.

51) The release of a beta particle by $^{14}_{6}C$ results in

   A) No change to the carbon
   B) $^{14}_{7}N$
   C) $^{16}_{8}O$
   D) $^{14}_{7}C$

The correct answer is B:) $^{14}_{7}N$. The reaction is $^{14}_{6}C \rightarrow ^{14}_{7}N + ^{0}_{-1}e$. Use the following information for the next two questions:

$H_2(g) + \frac{1}{2}O_2(g) \rightarrow H_2O(g)$ performed electrically using $Pt/H_2(g)/H^+ \| H_2O/O_2(g)/Pt$
Half cells: $H_2 \rightarrow 2H^+ + 2e^-$ $E^0 = +0.00$ V $O_2 + 4H^+ + 4e^- \rightarrow 2H_2O$ $E^0 = +1.23$ V

52) This half-reaction $H_2 \rightarrow 2H^+ + 2e^-$ indicates:

   A) Reduction at the anode
   B) Oxidation at the anode
   C) Reduction at the cathode
   D) Oxidation at the cathode

The correct answer is B:) Oxidation at the anode. H_2 is going from $0 \rightarrow +1$ so it is being oxidized at the anode.

53) Calculate the standard cell potential.

   A) 1.23 V
   B) + 1.23 V
   C) 2.46 V
   D) + 0.615

The correct answer is B:) + 1.23 V. The reaction: + 0.00 V + + 1.23 V = + 1.23 V.

54) The electron configuration notation for molybdenum is

   A) $1s^2\ 2s^2\ 2p^6\ 3s^2\ 3p^6\ 3d^{10}\ 4s^2\ 4p^6\ 4d^6$
   B) $1s^2\ 2s^2\ 2p^6\ 3s^2\ 3p^6\ 4s^2\ 3d^{10}\ 4p^6\ 3f^6$
   C) $1s^2\ 2s^2\ 2p^6\ 2d^{10}\ 3s^2\ 3p^6\ 3d^{10}\ 3f^4$
   D) $1s^2\ 2s^2\ 2p^6\ 3s^2\ 3p^6\ 4s^2\ 3d^{10}\ 4p^6\ 5s^2\ 4d^4$

The correct answer is D:) $1s^2\ 2s^2\ 2p^6\ 3s^2\ 3p^6\ 4s^2\ 3d^{10}\ 4p^6\ 5s^2\ 4d^4$. The order of filling is 1s 2s 2p 3s 3p 4s 3d 4p 5s 4d 5p 6s 4f 5d 6p 7s 5f 6d 7p with s sublevels holding a maximum of 2 electrons, p holding up to 6, d up to 10 and f up to 14.

55) As the number of neutrons in an atom of a given element increases, its atomic

　　A) Number increases
　　B) Number decreases
　　C) Mass increases
　　D) Mass decreases

The correct answer is C:) Mass increases. The atomic number is the number of protons while the atomic mass is the number of protons and neutrons.

56) An atom containing 4 protons, 5 neutrons and 3 electrons has an atomic mass of

　　A) 7 amu
　　B) 9 amu
　　C) 12 amu
　　D) 4 amu

The correct answer is B:) 9 amu. Protons and neutrons are each 1 amu. Electrons have no mass.

57) The periodic property which decreases all the way across the table is

　　A) Ionization energy
　　B) Atomic radius
　　C) Ionic size
　　D) Shielding effect

The correct answer is B:) Atomic radius. The atomic radius decreases all the way across the table since adding both protons and electrons going across giving a greater attraction of the electrons by the protons, so pull the electrons in tighter to the nucleus.

58) If 88.0% of the atoms of an element have a mass of 28.0 amu, 9.0% have a mass of 29.0 amu, and the rest have a mass of 30.0 amu, what is the average atomic mass?

　　A) 28.15 amu
　　B) 27.25 amu
　　C) 24.64 amu
　　D) 45.0 amu

The correct answer is A:) 28.15 amu. Average atomic mass = (0.88)(28.0) + (0.09)(29.0) + (0.03)(30.0) = 28.15 amu.

59) The sodium ion consists of

    A) 11 protons, 11 neutrons, 11 electrons
    B) 12 protons, 11 neutrons, 12 electrons
    C) 11 protons, 12 neutrons, 10 electrons
    D) 10 protons, 11 neutrons, 11 electrons

The correct answer is C:) 11 protons, 12 neutrons, 10 electrons. Sodium's atomic number is 11 so it has 11 protons. Its atomic mass is 22.99 so it has 22.99 – 11 = 11.99 or 12 neutrons. As an atom, it is neutral so it has the same number of electrons as protons, but as an ion, it loses the 3s1 electron, giving it 11 – 1 = 10 electrons.

60) According to modern methods of naming binary compounds, the name for P_4S_3 is

    A) Phosphoric sulfide
    B) Phosphorus sulfide
    C) Phosphorus trisulfide
    D) Tetraphosphorus trisulfide

The correct answer is D:) Tetraphosphorus trisulfide. It is made of two nonmetals, so the number of atoms of each element must be specified.

61) Copper (II) phosphate is

    A) Cu_2PO_4
    B) $Cu_3(PO_4)_2$
    C) $Cu_2(PO_4)_3$
    D) $CuPO_4$

The correct answer is B:) $Cu_3(PO_4)_2$. Copper (II) has a charge of +2 and phosphate (PO_4) has a charge of -3. Since it has to be neutral, three ions of Cu^{+2} are needed and two polyatomic ions of PO_4^{-3} are needed.

62) The two opposing forces at work in the nucleus of an atom are

    A) Electrostatic force and radiation
    B) Gravity and the nuclear strong force
    C) Nuclear strong force and electrostatic force
    D) Electrostatic force and gravity

The correct answer is C:) Nuclear strong force and electrostatic force. The nuclear strong force pulls together different atomic particles and the electrostatic force pushes apart the like charges of the protons in the nucleus.

63) The gram formula mass of $(NH_4)_2SO_4$ is

   A) 74 grams
   B) 118 grams
   C) 114 grams
   D) 132 grams

The correct answer is D:) 132 grams. 2 N + 2 (4 H) + S + 4 O = 2(14) + 8(1) + 1(32) + 4(16) = 28 + 8 + 32 + 64 = 132 grams.

64) Approximately how many moles of atoms are there in 48.09 grams of sulfur?

   A) 16.03 moles
   B) 0.667 moles
   C) 1.50 moles
   D) 1541.77 moles

The correct answer is C:) 1.50 moles. 48.09 g S x 1 mole S / 32.06 g S = 1.50 moles.

65) What is the density of UF_6?

   A) 22.4 liters
   B) 15.45 grams
   C) 352 grams/mole
   D) 15.45 grams/liter

The correct answer is D:) 15.45 grams/liter. Gram formula mass for UF_6 is (1)(238.03 grams U / 1 mole U) + (6)(18.00 grams F / 1 mole F) = 238.03 grams / mol + 108 grams / mol = 346.03 grams/mol UF_6. Density is expressed in grams/liter, so divide gfm by 22.4 liters/mol. (346.03 grams / mol) / (22.4 l / mol) = 15.45 g/l.

66) Calculate the empirical formula for the compound formed when 0.923 grams of sodium combines with hydrogen to produce 0.963 grams of compound.

   A) Na2H
   B) NaH
   C) Na2H2
   D) NaH2

The correct answer is B:) NaH. 0.923 g Na and 0.963 – 0.923 g H = 0.040 g H. Percent composition is (0.923/0.963)(100%) = 95.8% Na and (0.040/0.963)(100%) = 4.2%H To convert percentages to moles: For Na, (95.8 g NA) (1 mol Na / 23 g NA) = 4.17 OR 4.2 mol Na. For H, (4.2 g H)(1 mol H / 1 g H) = 4.2 mol H for a 1:1 ratio or NaH.

67) Ascorbic acid, also known as vitamin C, has a percentage composition of 40.9% carbon, 4.58% hydrogen, and 54.5% oxygen. Its molecular mass is 176.1 grams. What is its molecular formula?

   A) CH_2O
   B) $C_2H_2O_4$
   C) $C_3H_4O_3$
   D) $C_6H_8O_6$

The correct answer is D:) $C_6H_8O_6$. Convert percentages to moles: (40.9 gC)(1 mol C/12 gC) = 3.41 mol C; (4.58 g H)(1 mol H/1 g H) = 4.58 mol H; (54.5 g O)(1 mol O/16 g O) = 3.41 mol O. The C:O ratio is 1:1, but the C:H or O:H ratio is 3.41:4.58 which makes it 4.58/3.41 = 1.34 so all have to be multiplied by 3 to get the whole numbers of C:H:O = $C_3H_4O_3$ for an empirical formula. The mass of $C_3H_4O_3$ is (3) (12 g C/1 molC) + (4) (1 g H/1 mol H) + (3)(16 g O/1 mol O) = 36 g/mol C + 4 g/mol H + 48 g/mol O = 88 g/mol for $C_3H_4O_3$. The molecular mass/empirical mass = 176.1 g/88 g = 2, so multiply the subscripts by 2.

68) A nucleus spontaneously ejects a package of two protons and two neutrons. This type of radiation is referred to as

   A) Alpha decay
   B) Beta decay
   C) Gamma decay
   D) Delta decay

The correct answer is A:) Alpha decay. Alpha decay results in the atomic number dropping by two and the atomic mass dropping by four.

69) Oxygen is one of the most active elements as would be expected from its

   A) Low ionization energy
   B) High electronegativity
   C) High atomic radius
   D) High ionization energy

The correct answer is B:) High electronegativity. The higher the electronegativity, the more reactive the element.

70) The compound that contains 50% of each element by mass is

   A) CO
   B) CO_2
   C) Na_2O_2
   D) SO_2

The correct answer is D:) SO_2. The mass of S = 32 g/mole and the mass of O_2 is (2) (16 g/mole) = 32 g/mole.

71) In a balanced equation, the relative numbers of moles of the reactants used and products formed are given by

   A) Subscripts within parentheses
   B) Coefficients of the formulas
   C) Subscripts outside the parentheses
   D) Superscripts of the formulas

The correct answer is B:) Coefficients of the formulas. Subscripts balance formulas; coefficients balance equations.

72) An element has an atomic number of 4, an atomic mass of 6 and 4 electrons. It is a(n)

   A) Ion
   B) Cation
   C) Anion
   D) Isotope

The correct answer is D:) Isotope. Ion, cation and antion all deal with elements for which the number of protons and electrons are out of balance. In this case, it is the protons and neutrons that are out of balance, making it an isotope.

73) The algebraic sum of the oxidation numbers of the atoms in the formula of a radical is equal to its

   A) Charge
   B) Valence
   C) Positive charge
   D) Negative charge

The correct answer is A:) Charge. Some of the oxidation numbers will be positive and some will be negative, so when those are added together the resulting number (positive or negative) will be the charge on the radical.

74) Which type of radioactive decay is characterized by an increase of one in the atomic number, but no change in atomic mass?

   A) Alpha decay
   B) Beta decay
   C) Gamma decay
   D) Delta decay

The correct answer is B:) Beta decay. In beta decay, a neutron splits into a proton and an electron, and the electron is ejected. Therefore, the atomic mass wouldn't change but the atomic number would.

75) Products which are insoluble and leave the reaction environment are

   A) Perceptions
   B) Precepts
   C) Masses
   D) Precipitates

The correct answer is D:) Precipitates. A precipitate is a solid substance formed as a product of the reactants. It is insoluble in that environment and drops to the bottom of the beaker. It can be a salt, but is not always a salt. It is usually crystalline.

76) Which of the following is correct?

   A) $N_2 + 6 H \rightarrow 2 NH_3$
   B) $2 N + 3 H_2 \rightarrow 2 NH_3$
   C) $N + 3 H \rightarrow NH_3$
   D) $N_2 + 3 H_2 \rightarrow 2 NH_3$

The correct answer is D:) $N_2 + 3 H_2 \rightarrow 2 NH_3$. Synthesis reaction of nitrogen and hydrogen to form ammonia. Nitrogen and hydrogen are diatomic, N_2 and H_2, so cannot be single atoms of elements. Coefficients must be whole numbers. There must be two nitrogen atoms on each side of the arrow which means the six hydrogen atoms on the right must be balanced with six on the left.

77) Barium carbonate, when heated, yields

   A) Barium carbide and water
   B) Barium carbide and oxygen
   C) Barium and carbon dioxide
   D) Barium oxide and carbon dioxide

The correct answer is D:) Barium oxide and carbon dioxide. Decomposition of a carbonate: $Ba(CO_3) \rightarrow BaO + CO_2$.

78) Aluminum + iron(III) oxide →

   A) $Al_2(Fe_2O_3)_3$
   B) $Al_2O_3 + Fe$
   C) $Al_2O_3 + 2\ Fe$
   D) $Al_3O_2 + Fe$

The correct answer is C:) $Al_2O_3 + 2\ Fe$. Single replacement reaction: $2\ Al + Fe_2O_3 \rightarrow Al_2O_3 + 2\ Fe$.

79) $2\ Na + 2\ H_2O \rightarrow$

   A) $2\ NaOH + O_2\uparrow$
   B) $Na_2OH + H_2\uparrow$
   C) $Na(OH)_2 + H_2\uparrow$
   D) $2\ NaOH + H_2\uparrow$

The correct answer is D:) $2\ NaOH + H_2\uparrow$. A single replacement reaction involving water gives a hydroxide and hydrogen gas.

80) Ammonium sulfide + iron(II) nitrate →

   A) $NH_4NO_3 + FeS$
   B) $2\ NH_4NO_3 + FeS$
   C) $2\ NH_3NO_3 + Fe_3S_2$
   D) $(NH_4)2NO_3 + FeS$

The correct answer is B:) $2\ NH_4NO_3 + FeS$. Double displacement reaction: $(NH_4)2S + Fe(NO_3)2 \rightarrow 2\ NH_4NO_3 + FeS$.

81) How much force is required to accelerate a 50 kg weight at 20 m/s2 (assuming no other forces are involved)?

A) 70 N
B) 100 N
C) 500 N
D) 1000 N

The correct answer is D:) 1000 N. F = ma = (50 kg)(20 m/s$_2$) = 1000 N.

82) If 16 liters of carbon monoxide is burned to form carbon dioxide, how many liters of oxygen will be required and how many liters of carbon dioxide will be produced?

A) 16 L O_2 and 16 L CO_2
B) 16 L O_2 and 32 L CO_2
C) 8 L O_2 and 8 L CO_2
D) 8 L O_2 and 16 L CO_2

The correct answer is D:) 8 L O_2 and 16 L CO_2. The balanced equation: 2 CO + O_2 → 2 CO_2. Therefore, 16 liters CO x 1 mol O_2/2 mol CO = 8 liters O_2 and 16 liters CO x 2 mol CO_2/2 mol CO = 16 liters CO_2.

83) For the reaction of 7.0 moles of aluminum and 8.0 moles of chlorine, which will be the limiting reagent and by how much?

A) Chorine by 5.33 moles
B) Aluminum by 5.33 moles
C) Chlorine by 1.67 moles
D) Aluminum by 1.67 moles

The correct answer is C:) Chlorine by 1.67 moles. The balanced equation: 2 Al + 3 Cl_2 → 2 $AlCl_3$
7.0 mol Al x (2 mol $AlCl_3$/2 mol Al) = 7.0 mol $AlCl_3$
8.0 mol Cl_2 x (2 mol $AlCl_3$/3 mol Cl_2) = 5.33 mol $AlCl_3$ Chlorine is the limiting reagent by 7.0 – 5.33 = 1.67 moles.

84) Calcium carbonate can be decomposed by heating. What is the percent yield of this reaction if 24.8 grams of $CaCO_3$ is heated to give 13.1 grams of CaO?

A) 94.2%
B) 92.4%
C) 47.2%
D) 89.3%

The correct answer is A:) 94.2%. To calculate the theoretical yield, start with a balanced equation: $CaCO_3 \rightarrow CaO + CO_2$ 24.8 g $CaCO_3$ x 1 mol $CaCO_3$/100.08 g $CaCO_3$ x 1 mol/1mol CaO x 56.08 g CaO/1 mol CaO = 13.90 g CaO
Percent yield = actual yield / theoretical yield x 100% so Percent yield = 13.1 g/13.9 g x 100% = 94.2%.

85) Hydrazine, N_2H_4, is used as a rocket fuel. It reacts with oxygen to form nitrogen and water: N_2H_4 (l) + O_2(g) $\rightarrow$ N_2 (g) + 2 H_2O(g) How many liters of N_2 (at STP) form when 1.0 kg of N_2H_4 reacts with 1.0 kg O_2?

A) 0.70 L N_2
B) 46.17 L N_2
C) 700.0 L O_2
D) 700.0 L N_2

The correct answer is D:) 700.0 L N_2. kg N_2H_4 x (1000 g N_2H_4/1.0 kg N_2H_4) x (1 mol N_2H_4/30.02 g N_2H_4) x (1 mol N_2/1 mol N_2H_4) x (22.4 L N_2/1 mol N_2) = 746.17 L N_2 kg O_2 x (1000 g O_2/1.0 kg O_2) x (1 mol O_2/32.00 g O_2) x (1 mol N_2/1 mol O_2) x (22.4 L N_2/1mol N_2) = 700.0 L N_2 - limiting - what is produced.

86) If an object is being pulled with a force of 30 N and is accelerating at a rate of 10 m/s_2, what must be its mass (assuming no other forces are involved)?

A) 3 kg
B) 30 kg
C) 300 kg
D) 3000 kg

The correct answer is A:) 3 kg. F = ma, therefore m = F/a = (30 N)/(10m/s_2) = 3 kg.

87) A certain solution is found to contain 0.00001 mole of H_3O+ per liter. Its pH is

   A) 0.00001
   B) 1 x 10-5
   C) 5
   D) -5

The correct answer is C:) 5. 0.00001 = 1.0 x 10-5 mol/L which is a pH of 5.

88) $Ca(OH)_2$ is a(n)

   A) Arrhenius acid
   B) A salt
   C) Lewis acid
   D) Arrhenius base

The correct answer is D:) Arrhenius base. Arrhenius bases have to have OH- in them.

89) If a 1 kg object is being pulled to the left with an acceleration of 10 m/s_2, and being simultaneously pulled to the right with a force of 5 N, what is the resulting net force?

   A) -10 N
   B) -5 N
   C) 3 N
   D) Cannot be determined with information given

The correct answer is B:) -5 N. Net force is the sum of the forces acting on an object. In this case a negative (which in this case we define as to the left, though it is a matter of preference) force of (1kg)(10 m/s^2) or 10 N, and a positive force of 5 N. 5 N - 10 N = - 5 N.

90) An object that is falling in uniform motion under the power of gravity is said to be

   A) At rest
   B) In free fall
   C) Accelerating randomly
   D) None of the above

The correct answer is B:) In free fall. One of the most common situations in which kinematics equations are used is when an object is in freefall, which means that it is falling under the influence of gravity.

91) In the reaction $HNO_3 + H_2O \leftrightarrow H_3O^+ + NO_3^-$, which is NOT true? HNO_3 & NO_3^- are a conjugate acid-base pair

   A) H_2O is an acid
   B) H_2O & H_3O^+ are a conjugate acid-base pair
   C) H_2O is a hydrogen acceptor
   D) H_2O is a base

The correct answer is A:) H_2O is an acid. HNO_3 donates a H+ so it is an acid and pairs with NO_3^- as an acid-base pair. H_2O accepts a H+ so it is a base and pairs with H_3O^+ as an acid-base pair.

92) A 2 kg object is accelerated uniformly from rest to 10 m/s in 2 seconds. The force required to make this happen is

   A) 2 N
   B) 5 N
   C) 10 N
   D) Cannot be determined

The correct answer is C:) 10 N. In this problem the acceleration must be determined first. The acceleration is $(10-0)/2 = 5$ m/s^2. Then, using Newton's Second Law of Motion, F = ma = (2)(5) = 10 N.

93) The oxidation number of H in $Ba(OH)_2$ is

   A) +1
   B) -1
   C) -2
   D) 0

The correct answer is A:) +1. Hydrogen is always +1 except in a metal hydride such as NaH when it is -1.

94) In which of the following situations could the kinematics equations NOT be used?

   A) If an object had a mass greater than 100 kg.
   B) If an object were accelerating under the influence of gravity.
   C) If an object's acceleration varied with time.
   D) Kinematics equations are universally applicable.

The correct answer is C:) If an object's acceleration varied with time. The kinematics equations can only be used in situations with uniform motion – meaning the acceleration must be constant.

95) In the equation, $K_2Cr_2O_7 + H_2O + S \rightarrow KOH + Cr_2O_3 + SO_2$, the chromium ion makes what oxidation number change?

   A) +5 to +3
   B) +6 to +2
   C) +12 to +6
   D) +6 to +3

The correct answer is D:) +6 to +3. In $K_2Cr_2O_7$ the K is +1 (total +2) and the O is -2 (total -14), so the total Cr is +12, making each a +6. In Cr_2O_3 the O is -2 (total -6), so the Cr total is + 6, making each Cr +3.

96) Which of the following elements would be the least likely to bond with other elements?

   A) Carbon (atomic number 6)
   B) Oxygen (atomic number 8)
   C) Argon (atomic number 18)
   D) Aluminum (atomic number 13)

The correct answer is C:) Argon (atomic number 18). Argon has a full valence shell, making it less likely than the other elements to react.

97) How many milliliters of 0.28M $K_2Cr_2O_7$ are needed to reduce 1.40 g of sulfur in the equation in #84 (when balanced)?

   A) 156.3 mL
   B) 104.2 mL
   C) 2000 mL
   D) 2,402.6 mL

The correct answer is B:) 104.2 mL. Balanced equation: $2 K_2Cr_2O_7 + 2 H_2O + 3 S \rightarrow 4 KOH + 2 Cr_2O_3 + 3 SO_2$
(1.40 g S)(1 mol S/32.0 g S)(2 mol $K_2Cr_2O_7$ / 3 mol S)(1L $K_2Cr_2O_7$/0.28 mol $K_2Cr_2O_7$)(1000 mL/1L) = 104.2 mL.

98) A .5 kg rock is dropped from rest out of a hot air balloon that is 20 meters in the air. Ignoring air friction, how long will it take to hit the ground?

   A) 1 s
   B) 2 s
   C) 4 s
   D) 5 s

The correct answer is B:) 2 s. Using the second of the kinematics equations: $\Delta x = (1/2) at^2 + v t$ means that we can determine $20 = (1/2)(9.8)t^2 + (0)t$. Solving for t: $t^2 \approx 4$ and t = 2.

99) What are the correct coefficients in the correct order for this redox equation: $HNO_3 + H_2S \rightarrow S + NO + H_2O$

   A) 1, 1, 1, 2, 1
   B) 2, 3, 3, 2, 4
   C) 2, 1, 1, 2, 1
   D) 2, 1, 1, 1, 2

The correct answer is B:) 2, 3, 3, 2, 4. In HNO_3, H = +1, O = -2 (total -6), so N = +5. In H_2S, H = +1 and S = -2. On the right, S = 0. If O = -2, then N = +2. In H_2O, H = +1 and O = -2. The two half-reactions are: $N^{+5} \rightarrow N^{+2}$ and $S^{-2} \rightarrow S^0$. By adding $3e^-$ to N^{+5} and $2e^-$ to S^0 the half-reactions are: $N^{+5} + 3e^- \rightarrow N^{+2}$ and $S^{-2} \rightarrow S^0 + 2e^-$ so the N's must be multiplied by 2 and the S's by 3. The balanced equation: $2 HNO_3 + 3 H_2S \rightarrow 3 S + 2 NO + 4 H_2O$.

Use this equation to answer the next two questions:

$2 Sb(s) + HNO_3(aq) \rightarrow Sb_2O_5(s) + NO(g) + H_2O(l)$

100) An object is moving such that v = 5 and a = -5. Which of the following describes its motion?

    A) It must be speeding up because velocity is positive
    B) It must be slowing down because acceleration is negative
    C) It must be speeding up because acceleration and velocity are in opposite directions
    D) It must be slowing down because acceleration and velocity are in opposite directions

The correct answer is D:) It must be slowing down because acceleration and velocity are in opposite directions. A negative acceleration does not always indicate decreasing velocity. Rather, it is the relationship between the acceleration and velocity that determines this.

101) What element is oxidized?

    A) Sb
    B) H
    C) N
    D) O

The correct answer is A:) Sb. $Sb0 \rightarrow Sb2+5$ Oxidation shows an increase in oxidation number.

102) The following data is collected as a car accelerates through an intersection. Determine its average acceleration from t=1 to t=3.

v (m/s):	0	2	4	6	8
t (s):	1	2	3	4	5

    A) 1 m/s^2
    B) 2 m/s^2
    C) 3 m/s^2
    D) Cannot be determined

The correct answer is B:) 2 m/s^2. Average acceleration = $[v(3)-v(1)]/3-1 = (4-0)/2 = 2 \text{ m/s}^2$.

103) What is the oxidizing agent?

A) Sb
B) HNO$_3$
C) H
D) O

The correct answer is B:) HNO$_3$. N^{+5} → N^{+2} Nitrogen is reduced. The compound containing the element which is reduced is the oxidizing agent.

104) The volume of a particular amount of dry gas is inversely proportional to the pressure, provided the temperature remains constant is

A) Charles' Law
B) Boyle's Law
C) Kelvin's Law
D) James' Law

The correct answer is B:) Boyle's Law. Boyle's Law states that for a given mass of gas at constant temperature, the volume of the gas varies inversely with pressure.

105) Sam pushes a 10 kg block with an acceleration of 3 m/s2 for 4 seconds covering a distance of 24 m. Tom pushes a 12 kg block with an acceleration of 5 m/s2 for 2 seconds covering 10 m. Which of the two boys deliver the most power how much did he deliver?

A) Sam, 720 W
B) Sam, 180 W
C) Tom, 600 W
D) Tom, 300 W

The correct answer is D:) Tom, 300 W.

106) An object with an initial velocity of 5 m/x moves with a constant acceleration of 4 m/s^2 for twelve seconds. What is its final velocity?

A) 20 m/s
B) 31 m/s
C) 44 m/s
D) 53 m/s

The correct answer is D:) 53 m/s. This can be determined using the first kinematics equation: $v = v_o + at = 5 + (4)(12) = 5 + 48 = 53$ m/s.

107) Given 700 mL of oxygen at 7° C and 80.0 cm pressure, what volume does it have at 27° C and 50.0 cm pressure?

   A) 469 mL
   B) 1045 mL
   C) 1200 mL
   D) 0.112 mL

The correct answer is C:) 1200 mL. $P_1V_1T_2 = P_2V_2T_1$ (80.0 cm)(700 mL)(27 + 273) = (50.0 cm)(x)(7 + 273) therefore: (1.68 x 107) = (1.40 x 104) (x), so 1200 mL = x.

108) The catalyst in a reaction does NOT

   A) Increase the rate of the reaction
   B) Interfere with the reaction
   C) Lower the activation energy barrier
   D) Get recovered at the end

The correct answer is B:) Interfere with the reaction. The catalyst does increase the rate of the reaction, lower its activation energy barrier, and get recovered at the end of the reaction.

109) In the reaction $HCl + NaOH \rightarrow NaCl + H_2O$

   A) NaCl will be a precipitate
   B) Na+ will be a spectator ion
   C) NaCl will be an acid
   D) H_2O will be a base

The correct answer is A:) NaCl will be a precipitate. This is an acid-base reaction resulting in a precipitated salt and water.

110) Which of the following describes the property of refraction?

   A) Light will "bounce" off of smooth surfaces like glass or mirrors.
   B) Light will change speed and direction when it changes mediums.
   C) Light will bend slightly as it passes around an object.
   D) None of the above

The correct answer is B:) Light will change speed and direction when it changes mediums.

111) In liquids dissolved in liquids, little change in temperature is expected because

   A) Only a small amount of solute can dissolve
   B) All liquids are completely miscible
   C) No change in physical state occurs
   D) Hydration prevents chemical activity

The correct answer is C:) No change in physical state occurs. No heat is given off or required to make a phase change.

112) A precipitate is formed when a dilute solution of H_2SO_4 is added to

   A) Na^+
   B) K^+
   C) Al_3^+
   D) Ca_2^+

The correct answer is D:) Ca_2^+. Most sulfate salts are soluble, but $BaSO_4$, $PbSO_4$, and $CaSO_4$ form precipitates.

113) A sample of a vapor having a mass of 0.519 grams occupies 123 mL at 100° C and 745 mm Hg. What is its molecular weight?

   A) 0.002 g/mol
   B) 131.7 g/mol
   C) 11.6 g/mol
   D) 94.5 g/mol

The correct answer is B:) 131.7 g/mol. Using PV = nRT, substitute the numbers to get (745 mm)(1 atm/760 mm)(0.123 L) = (0.519 g / x mol)(0.082 L-atm/K-mol)(100 + 273 K) which is (0.121 atm-L)(x mol) = 15.87 g-L-atm to give x – 131.7 g/mol.

114) What is NOT true of buffers?

   A) They take advantage of common ions
   B) They are derived from a weak acid and one of its salts
   C) A buffer solution can resist drastic pH changes
   D) Buffers are made of a weak acid and a weak base

The correct answer is D:) Buffers are made of a weak acid and a weak base.

115) Triple point refers to the point at which

   A) The heat of vaporization, the heat of fusion, and the boiling point are equal
   B) A solid turns into a gas without becoming a liquid
   C) The heat of fusion equals the heat of vaporization
   D) Solid, liquid and gas are in equilibrium

The correct answer is D:) Solid, liquid and gas are in equilibrium. The triple point is the temperature and pressure at which solid, liquid and gas are in equilibrium.

116) Sam pushes a 10 kg block with an acceleration of 3 m/s² for 4 seconds covering a distance of 24 m. Tom pushes a 12 kg block with an acceleration of 5 m/s² for 2 seconds covering 10 m. Which of the two boys did the most work and how much did he do?

   A) Sam, 30 J
   B) Tom, 60 J
   C) Sam, 720 J
   D) Tom, 600 J

The correct answer is C:) Sam, 720 J. Sam did (10 kg)(3 m/s²)(24 m)= 720 J of work with (720 J)/(4 z) = 180 watts of power. Tom did (12 kg)(5 m/s²)(10 m)= 600 J of work with (600 J)/(2 s) = 300 watts of power.

117) It was found that 85.5 g of a nonelectrolyte dissolved in 1 kg of water lowered the freezing point of water 0.465 C. The molecular weight of the solute is

   A) 171 g/mol
   B) 342 g/mol
   C) 85.5 g/mol
   D) 34.2 g/mol

The correct answer is B:) 342 g/mol. Use the equation: $\Delta T_f = K_f m$
0.465° C = 1.86° C/m (m) 0.25 m = m = 0.25 mol/kg to get (85.5 g/1 kg)/(0.25 mol/kg) = 342 g/mol.

118) Which of the following is an example of refraction?

   A) Interference patterns of waves
   B) Rainbows
   C) Mirrors
   D) A pencil appearing to bend in the water

The correct answer is D:) A pencil appearing to bend in the water. Refraction is that light will change speed and direction when it changes mediums, which results in the pencil appearing bent.

119) A hypothesis must

   A) Explain all types of experiences
   B) Use mathematics
   C) Be able to be tested by inductive reasoning
   D) Be able to be tested by designed experiments

The correct answer is D:) Be able to be tested by designed experiments. A hypothesis must be testable by observation, usually by experimentation to seek exceptions or draw supporting conclusions.

120) A reaction that gives off heat is

   A) Exothermic
   B) Stable
   C) Endothermic
   D) Catalyzed

The correct answer is A:) Exothermic. An exothermic reaction gives off energy in the form of heat.

121) Which of the following changes occurs to light when it changes the medium it is moving through?

   A) Speed
   B) Direction
   C) Frequency
   D) Both A and B

The correct answer is D:) Both A and B. This property is referred to as refraction.

122) How much power is required to do 500 J of work in 5 seconds?

A) 2500 W
B) 250 W
C) 200 W
D) 100 W

The correct answer is D:) 100 W . P = W/t = 500/(5) = 100 W.

 Test-Taking Strategies

Here are some test-taking strategies that are specific to this test and to other DSST tests in general:
- Keep your eyes on the time. Pay attention to how much time you have left.
- Read the entire question and read all the answers. Many questions are not as hard to answer as they may seem. Sometimes, a difficult sounding question really only is asking you how to read an accompanying chart. Chart and graph questions are on most DANTES/DSST tests and should be an easy free point.
- If you don't know the answer immediately, the new computer-based testing lets you mark questions and come back to them later if you have time.
- Read the wording carefully. Some words can give you hints to the right answer. There are no exceptions to an answer when there are words in the question such as always, all or none. If one of the answer choices includes most or some of the right answers, but not all, then that is not the answer. Here is an example:

> The primary colors include all of the following:
> A) Red, Yellow, Blue, Green
> B) Red, Green, Yellow
> C) Red, Orange, Yellow
> D) Red, Yellow, Blue

Although item A includes all the right answers, it also includes an incorrect answer, making it incorrect. If you didn't read it carefully, were in a hurry, or didn't know the material well, you might fall for this.
- Make a guess on a question that you do not know the answer to. There is no penalty for an incorrect answer. Eliminate the answer choices that you know are incorrect. For example, this will let your guess be a 1 in 3 chance instead.

 # Test Preparation

How much you need to study depends on your knowledge of a subject area. If you are interested in literature, took it in school, or enjoy reading then your study and preparation for the literature or humanities test will not need to be as intensive as that of someone who is new to literature.

This book is much different than the regular DANTES study guides. This book actually teaches you the information that you need to know to pass the test. If you are particularly interested in an area, or feel that you want more information, do a quick search online. We've tried not to include too much depth in areas that are not as essential on the test. Everything in this book will be on the test. It is important to understand all major theories and concepts listed in the table of contents. It is also important to know any bolded words.

Don't worry if you do not understand or know a lot about the area. With minimal study, you can complete and pass the test.

One of the fallacies of other test books is test questions. People assume that the content of the questions are similar to what will be on the test. That is not the case. They are only there to test your "test taking skills" so for those who know to read a question carefully, there is not much added value from taking a "fake" test.

To prepare for the test, make a series of goals. Allot a certain amount of time to review the information you have already studied and to learn additional material. Take notes as you study; it will help you learn the material.

 # Legal Note

All rights reserved. This Study Guide, Book and Flashcards are protected under the US Copyright Law. No part of this book or study guide or flashcards may be reproduced, distributed or stored in a retrieval system, or transmitted in any form or by any means, electronic, mechanical, photocopying, recording, or otherwise, without the prior written permission of the publisher Breely Crush Publishing, LLC.

FLASHCARDS

This section contains flashcards for you to use to further your understanding of the material and test yourself on important concepts, names or dates. Read the term or question then flip the page over to check the answer on the back. Keep in mind that this information may not be covered in the text of the study guide. Take your time to study the flashcards, you will need to know and understand these concepts to pass the test.

Meter	**Liter**
Gram	**Dynamics**
Force	**s = d/t**
Displacement	**Inertia**

Measure of volume	Measure of length
The study of the relationship between motion and the forces affecting motion	Measure of mass
speed=distance/time	Causes motion to start or to stop, to change direction, or to change speed
The tendency of a moving object to keep moving	When a body moves from one location to another

Newton's first law of motion	**Newton's second law of motion**
$F = ma$	**Newton's third law**
$M = mv$	**Centripetal force**
Energy	**Law of Conservation of Energy**

That if a net force acts on an object, it will cause the object to accelerate	An object at rest will remain at rest and an object in motion will remain in motion at a constant velocity unless acted upon by an external force
For every action there is an equal and opposite reaction	Force=mass x acceleration
The force necessary to keep an object moving in a circle	Momentum=mass x velocity
Energy cannot be created or destroyed; it may be transformed from one form into another, but the total amount of energy never changes	The ability to exert a force through a distance or to do work

Kinetic energy	Potential energy
Name the six simple machines	A wedge is how many inclined planes?
Temperature	Heat
Thermometers	Freezing point for celsius

Stored energy	Energy of motion
Two	(1) lever, (2) pulley, (3) wheel and axle, (4) inclined plane, (5) screw, and (6) wedge
The total internal energy of the material	A measure of the average kinetic energy of the particles in a material
0 degrees	Used to measure temperature

Boiling point for celsius	**Freezing point for Fahrenheit**
Boiling point for Fahrenheit	**Calorie**
Kilocalorie	**BTU**
Heat transfer	**Heat Capacity**

32 degrees	100 degrees
Amount of energy that it takes to raise one gram of water one degree Celsius	212 degrees
British thermal unit	The amount of energy that it takes to raise one kilogram of water by one degree Celsius
The amount of heat energy that it takes to raise the temperature of a unit mass of the object by one degree	Heat energy that is transferred into or out of a system

Convection	**Radiation**
Reversible systems	**Reversible systems**
Thermodynamics Law #2	**Four states of matter**
Einstein's law of special relativity	**Speed of Light**

Heat transfer as the result of electromagnetic waves rather than moving particles	Heat transported by the movement of a heated liquid or gas
Energy can be neither created nor destroyed. It can be converted but you cannot increase the amount of energy in the universe or decrease it. The second part of the first law is that the change in internal energy of any system is equal to heat plus work.	Systems that are nearly always in a state of equilibrium
Solids, liquids, gases, and plasmas	There is a finite amount of energy in the universe, its quality is degraded irreversibly. Every time a chemical reaction takes place, part of the energy required to do the work is transformed into some other form than that which helped perform the work.
The speed of light is the speed with which one photon travels through time and space. In a vacuum, a photon will travel 3×10^8 m/s^{-1}	Neither distance nor time are absolute

Electromagnetic Radiation	**High frequency sound**
Age of the universe?	**Molecules are the building blocks of what?**
Atomic number	**Periodic Table of Elements**
Mass number	**Isotope**

High pitched	This radiation is a combination of oscillating electric and magnetic fields. They are normally perpendicular to each other through space and carry energy from one place to another. Light is one form of electromagnetic radiation.
Any living cell	12 billion years
The periodic table of elements is a classification system developed by a man named Mendeleev based upon the chemical properties of elements	In the periodic table of elements, the atomic number is always representative of the number of protons contained in the nucleus of an atom
An isotope is an atom with the same atomic number as an element, but a different mass number	The mass number of any atom is the number of protons plus the number of neutrons present in the nucleus of an atom. In other words, mass number equals the total number of particles present in the nucleus.

www.ingramcontent.com/pod-product-compliance
Lightning Source LLC
Chambersburg PA
CBHW081832300426
44116CB00014B/2558